HOPE FOR THE SEPARATED

HOPE FOR THE SEPARATED

by

GARY D. CHAPMAN

MOODY PRESS

CHICAGO

The author and publisher wish to express appreciation for
permission to reprint from the following:

"The Road Not Taken." From THE POETRY OF ROBERT
FROST, edited by Edward Connery Lathem. Copyright 1916.
Copyright 1969 by Holt, Rinehart and Winston. Copyright
1944 by Robert Frost. Reprinted by permission of Holt, Rinehart and Winston, Publishers.

"My Wonderful Lord," by Haldor Lillenas. Copyright 1938 by
Nazarene Publishing House. Used by permission.

Library of Congress Cataloging in Publication Data

Chapman, Gary D., 1938-
   Hope for the separated.
   Bibliography: p. 115.
   1. Divorce—Moral and religious aspects. 2. Marriage—Moral
and religious aspects. 3. Reconciliation. I. Title.

HQ824.C49   306.8'9   81-18667
ISBN 0-8024-3616-1   AACR2

20

Printed in the United States of America

Acknowledgments

I am deeply indebted to the many separated individuals who have shared their struggles with me. Out of the midst of the ambivalent feelings of love and hate, relief and pain, anger and concern, I have seen many of them seek the high road of reconciliation. Not all have succeeded, but all have matured. I have watched them deal responsibly with failure and rise to face the future with confidence. Their example has served to encourage me in the writing of this volume, which is designed to point the way to hope.

Sincere appreciation is expressed to Debbie Barr and Mary Hix, both of whom gave liberally of their expertise in editing and typing the manuscript.

Contents

Introduction

"We have a problem," a friend told me on the phone. "My wife's sister told us that her husband just left and is asking for a divorce. I know she is going to turn to me for advice, and I'm not sure what to tell her. Should she contest the divorce? How do we help her? What shall we say? We've never faced this in our family before!"

I asked some questions, gave some advice, and walked back to my study convinced that this book must be written.

Thousands of people experienced marital separation last year. I am certain that many of them sincerely want to know, "What should I do, as a Christian?" This book is an attempt to answer that question. It does not contain easy answers or rigid formulas. There is no simple medication for a marriage diseased to the point of separation. But for those who really want help, even if the medicine is "hard to swallow," read on. Your chances of recovery are good.

For pastors, lay counselors, and relatives who want to help those in the throes of separation, I have sought to give practical, biblical answers in language that everyone can understand. A number of helpful books have been written for the divorcee, but none, in my opinion, deal adequately with the individual's struggle during the separation period.

It is not to be assumed that separation always leads to divorce. Separation may just as well lead to a restored, enriched, growing marriage. The individuals involved must determine the outcome of separation. In this book we want to look realistically at both alternatives. Separation is not permanent. It is a time of transition leading to either resurrection or death. In either event, we must make the most of the process.

The assignments at the conclusion of each chapter will help you take specific steps toward incorporating ideas into your life. Ultimate value comes not in reading but in *applying* truth. An ancient sage once said, "The journey of a thousand miles begins with one step!"

I hope this book will help you take that step.

1

What Happened to Our Dream?

To separate or not to separate, that was the question. That question was settled when one of you left and took up residence at a separate location. Clothes and personal belongings may not have been moved, but you are living apart. The very word may bring fear to your heart, and you may not like it, but you are *separated,* and you may as well say it: "I am separated."

Separation is not death, although it is most certainly the "valley of the shadow of death" (Psalm 23:4). It is so near death that you may feel the same grief and pain experienced by those who release a loved one to death. But the shadow of death is not to be equated with death itself. Separation may be the valley of restoration, and the pain you feel may be the labor pains that will give rebirth to your marriage. On the other hand, separation may be the beginning of the end. The fruit of your separation will be determined by what you and your spouse say and do in the next few weeks and months.

In a very real sense, separation calls for intensive care, much like that given to one in grave physical danger. The condition of your marriage is "critical." Things can go either way at any moment. Proper medication is essential, which is the purpose of this book. Surgery may be required. That will call for the services of a counselor or pastor. What you do in the next few weeks will determine the quality of your life for years to come. Be assured, God is concerned about the outcome. You can count on Him for supernatural help.

Separation is not the time to capitulate. The battle for marital unity is not over until the death certificate is signed. In most states you have six to twelve months in which to wage war on the enemy of your marriage. The dreams and hopes you shared when you got married are still worth fighting for. You married each other because you were in love (or thought you were at the time). You dreamed of the perfect marriage in which each made the other supremely happy. What happened to that dream? What went wrong? What can you do to correct it?

The dream can live again. But not without work—work that will demand listening, understanding, discipline, and change—work that can result in the joy of a dream come true.

I know some of you are saying, "It sounds good, but it won't work. We've tried before. Besides, I don't think my spouse will even try again."

Perhaps you are right, but do not assume that the hostile attitude of your spouse will remain forever. One of the gifts of God to all men and women is the gift of choice. We can change, and that change can be for the better. Your spouse may be saying, "I'm through. It is finished. I don't want to talk about it!" Two weeks or two months from now, however, your mate may be willing to talk. Much depends on what you do in the meantime, and much depends on his or her response to the Spirit of God.

Others of you are saying, "I'm not sure that I want to work on this marriage. I've tried. I've given and given. It won't work, and I may as well get out now!" I am deeply sympathetic with those feelings. I know that when we have tried again and again without success, we may lose our desire to try once more. We see no hope, so we conclude that we have no alternative but to give up. Our emotions no longer encourage us to work on the marriage. That is why I never ask people, "Do you *want* to work on your marriage?" I always ask, *"Will* you work on your marriage?" At the point of separation, we have lost much of our "want to." We must now rely upon our will and not our emotions. We must remember our values, our commitments, our dreams, and we must choose to do what must be done to be true to them.

Where shall we go for help? For those who are Christians, there is one stable source to which we turn when we need guidance. That source is the Bible. Non-Christians may or may not turn to the Bible, but the Christian is drawn by the Spirit of God to the Scriptures. In the Bible we find not only what we ought to do but also the encouragement to do it. Even the non-Christian who sincerely seeks help in the Bible can find meaning in Paul's statement, "I can do all things through [Christ] who strengthens me" (Philippians 4:13). When we come to Christ, we find the outside help we need to do what our own resources are inadequate to accomplish.

When we turn to the Bible we see two road signs: one marked Detour, the other Wrong Way. On the sign marked Wrong Way appears the word *divorce*. On the sign marked Detour are the words *marital unity*. Let us explore the meaning and direction of those two signs.

According to the Old and New Testaments, divorce always represents the wrong way. In the beginning, when God told Adam and Eve, "Be fruitful and multiply, and fill the earth" (Genesis 1:28), He never gave the slightest hint that the marital relationship was to be anything but lifelong. The first mention of divorce in the Bible is found in the writings of Moses hundreds of years after man's creation (Leviticus 21:14, 22:13; Numbers 30:9; Deuteronomy 24:1-4). Moses permitted divorce, but it was never condoned or encouraged by God. Jesus later explained to the Pharisees that Moses had permitted divorce only because of their "hardness of heart" (Matthew 19:8) but that from the beginning divorce was not God's plan. Jesus affirmed that God's intention was monogamous, lifelong marital relationships. When God instituted marriage, divorce

13

was not an option. God did not create divorce any more than He created polygamy. Those were man's innovations. In God's sight those innovations are always clearly wrong.

On the other hand, the sign marked Detour—Marital Unity indicates that you have not lost sight of the goal, nor are you off the road. Rather, you are taking the circuitous route of separation because the bridge of your togetherness has collapsed. The detour sign may bring an immediate feeling of distress, but behind distress lies hope. There are at least signs to point you back to the main route. If you will follow carefully, the chances of finding your way are good.

Separation is like standing at a fork in the road of your life. You must choose which path you will follow in the next months. We have seen that God never encourages divorce, but He still allows man the freedom to choose either route. In the course of human history, man has made many unwise decisions. God has not immediately destroyed man for his wrong. Had God chosen that recourse, man would have been extinct thousands of years ago. God has allowed man genuine freedom—including freedom to curse God and walk his own way. The Bible indicates that, to one degree or another, we have all used that freedom to our own undoing (Isaiah 53:6).

The principle God instituted along with man's freedom is found in Galatians 6:7: "Do not be deceived, God is not mocked; for whatever a man sows, this he will also reap." God has simply allowed man to reap the harvest from the seed he plants, hoping that man will learn to plant good seed. "The one who sows to please his sinful nature, from that nature will reap destruction; the one who sows to please the Spirit, will reap eternal life" (Galatians 6:8, NIV*).

God's plans for man are good. God never instituted anything designed to make man miserable. " 'For I know the plans that I have for you,' declares the LORD, 'plans for welfare and not for calamity to give you a future and a hope' " (Jeremiah 29:11). When God says divorce is the wrong way He is not trying to

*New International Version.

14

make life difficult. He is pointing the way to prosperity and hope.

"But we did not have prosperity and hope before we separated," you say. That may be true, but past failure need not dictate the future. The lack of fulfillment you experienced before separation probably came from one of three sources: (1) lack of an intimate relationship with God, (2) lack of an intimate relationship with your mate, or (3) lack of an intimate understanding and acceptance of yourself. The first and last of those can be corrected without the aid of your spouse. The second, of course, will require the cooperation of both husband and wife. Radical change in all three areas is highly possible. Thus, the potential for the rebirth of your marriage is assured.

In later chapters I want to share ways of initiating change in each of the above areas. But first, I want to state clearly that the biblical ideal for a separated couple calls for reconciliation. You may not feel like reconciling. You may see no hope for reunion. The process may frighten you, but may I challenge you to follow the example of God Himself?

Throughout the Bible, God is pictured as having a love relationship with His people, in the Old Testament with Israel and in the New Testament with the church. On numerous occasions God has found Himself separated from His people, not of His choosing but of theirs. In a sense, the entire Bible is a record of God's attempts to be reconciled to His people. The book of Hosea gives the most graphic picture of the process.

Gomer, Hosea's wife, was unfaithful time and time again, but God said, "Go again, love [your wife], . . . even as the LORD loves the sons of Israel, though they turn to other gods . . ." (Hosea 3:1). Hosea was to be a picture of God's reaching out to Israel for reconciliation. In spite of Israel's idolatry and unfaithfulness to God, He said, "Therefore, behold, I will allure her, bring her into the wilderness, and speak kindly to her. Then I will give her her vineyards from there, and the valley of Achor [trouble] as a door of hope. And she will sing there as in the days of her youth, as in the day when she came up from the land of Egypt" (Hosea 2:14-15).

15

In the New Testament we hear Jesus express the pain of separation when He says, "O Jerusalem, Jerusalem, who kills the prophets and stones those who are sent to her! How often I wanted to gather your children together, the way a hen gathers her chicks under her wings, and you were unwilling. Behold, your house is being left to you desolate!" (Matthew 23:37-38).

In the book of Jeremiah, God says to Israel: "I remember . . . the devotion of your youth . . . your following after me through the wilderness, through a land not sown" (2:2). God goes on to describe how He protected Israel from her enemies during those days. But then came the coldness, the separation. "Can a virgin forget her ornaments, a bride her [wedding] attire? Yet My people have forgotten Me days without number" (2:32). " 'As a woman treacherously departs from her lover [husband], so you have dealt treacherously [unfaithfully] with Me, O house of Israel,' declares the LORD" (3:20).

The remainder of the book is a plea for reconciliation: " 'Return, faithless Israel,' declares the LORD, 'I will frown on you no longer, for I am merciful,' declares the LORD, 'I will not be angry forever. Only acknowledge your guilt—you have rebelled against the LORD your God, you have scattered your favors to foreign gods . . . Return, faithless people,' declares the LORD, 'for I am your husband' " (3:12-14, NIV).

Note that God always pleads for reconciliation on the basis of correcting sinful behavior. Never does God agree to reconcile while Israel continues in sin. "Return, faithless people; I will cure you of backsliding . . ." (3:22, NIV). " 'If you will return, O Israel,' declares the LORD, 'then you should return to Me. And if you will put away your detested things [idols] from My presence, and will not waver [go astray], and you will swear, "As the LORD lives," in truth, in justice, and in righteous; then the nations will bless themselves in Him and in Him they will glory' " (4:1-2).

There can be no reconciliation without repentance. In the marital relationship there must be mutual repentance, for almost always the failure has involved both parties. We will explore that further in later chapters, but the point I want to

16

establish here is that the biblical challenge calls us to seek repentance and reconciliation.

The purpose of this chapter is not to minimize the hurt, pain, frustration, anger, resentment, loneliness, and disappointment you may feel. Nor is it to take lightly your past efforts at marital adjustment. Instead, the purpose is to call you to accept the challenge of being separated, and to make the most of that challenge.

Sometimes separation brings a sense of emotional peace to the individual. That peace is mistakenly interpreted as an indication that separation and divorce must be right. One husband said, "This is the first week of peace I have had in years." Such peace is the result of removing yourself from the scene of battle. Naturally you have peace; you have left the conflict! Retreat, however, is never the road to victory. You must come from that retreat with renewed determination to defeat the enemy of your marriage.

Separation removes you from some of the constant pressure of conflict. It allows time for you to examine biblical principles for building a meaningful marriage. It permits self-examination in which emotions can be separated from behavior. It may stimulate a depth of openness in your communication that was not present before. In short, it places you in an arena where you can develop a new understanding of yourself and your spouse. Separation is not necessarily the beginning of the end. It may be only the beginning.

GROWTH ASSIGNMENTS

1. If you are the one who left, try to identify your reasons for leaving. Write those on a sheet of paper, completing the sentence: "I left because . . ."
2. Analyze each of those reasons. Which of those could be corrected if you or your mate chose to do so?
3. If you are the one left behind, try to identify the reasons your spouse left. Write those on a sheet of paper, completing the sentence: "I think he/she left because . . ."

4. Analyze each of those reasons. Which of those could be corrected if you or your mate chose to do so?
5. Read the next chapter with an open mind. Examine your attitudes and actions.

2

Taking Constructive Action

I want to begin this chapter by asking a very personal question, the same question I would ask if you were sitting in my office: *Will* you work on being reconciled to your spouse? *Will* you spend some energy, effort, and time finding out what can be done and then take constructive action? If you *will,* then I want to share some guideposts that I think will point the way.

EMOTIONS, ATTITUDES, AND ACTIONS

Bill and Martha have been separated for three months. He comes over once a week to visit with Susie, their five-year-old. Sometimes he will take Susie out for dinner, and sometimes Martha will invite him to eat with them. Most of the time he refuses her offer, but twice he has accepted. Martha tries hard to be positive, but inevitably she finds herself accusing Bill of seeing someone else, and from that point the conversation degenerates.

Before long she is saying the now oft-repeated words, "How could you do this to me? Do you have no self-respect or dignity? How do you think it makes me feel? How do you think it makes Susie feel? Don't think she doesn't know what's going on! She may be young, but she knows what you are doing. You are humiliating us. Your brother told me that he saw you on Thursday night. If you think for one minute that I am going to put up with this. . . . Then you come over here and act like everything is all right. Well, everything is not all right, and I want you to know it!" After a few more familiar and ill-chosen words she begins to cry and is soon sobbing uncontrollably.

Bill vacillates between retaliation and withdrawal. When he chooses to retaliate he can be as verbal as she, but silence is his usual response, and he leaves while she is still sobbing. Martha takes that as further rejection, and her hostility increases. Obviously, the road of separation is not leading them to reconciliation. If they continue that behavior they will be divorced.

Without realizing it, Martha may be accomplishing exactly the opposite of what she wants. She has become a slave to her hostile emotions and negative attitudes. She makes their time together extremely unpleasant. Her behavior is not designed to stimulate his return, but to drive him away. What man in his right mind would ever want to come back to a woman behaving in such a manner? I am not saying he *cannot* return, for he can in spite of her behavior. (More on Bill later.) Martha, however, is not working toward restoration, but toward a wider separation.

We cannot determine our emotions, but we can choose our attitudes and actions. Negative emotions need to be acknowledged but not served. A better approach for Martha would be to say, "Bill, I feel very angry and hurt when I think that you are seeing someone else. My friends say that they have seen you with someone, but you say that it is untrue. I'm confused. I want to believe you, but based upon the past, I have a hard time believing. At any rate, you know how strongly I feel about the idea. We can never get back together while you are having an affair. You will have to make that decision. In the meantime, I do not want to be controlled by my anger. I will try to treat you with dignity and respect. You are a person about whom I care very much. With God's help, I will not spend our time attacking you." Martha is now emotionally free to be a constructive influence on Bill. She has admitted her feelings but is not controlled by them.

What about Bill? What are his feelings and thoughts? He may feel very unloved and may have angry, hostile feelings against Martha based upon her past behavior. Those feelings also need to be acknowledged. His behavior may stem from an "I'll pay her back" attitude. He may reason, "She did not meet my needs for affection, so I was forced to turn elsewhere." Thus, he blames Martha for his behavior.

What will Bill do if he chooses to work on reconciliation? He might begin by identifying and acknowledging his own emotions. He might say to Martha, "I have felt for a long time that you really do not love me. I have felt rejected again and again through the years. I have felt that you demanded many things from me, but gave me little of your affection. So I feel angry and cold toward you. I hope that those feelings can be changed. I pray that we can learn to share openly with each other. I do not want to be controlled by my negative feelings."

Bill must then be honest about the nature of his relationship with other women. If he has romantic feelings toward someone else, those must be discussed. Reconciliation must always begin where we are. Romantic feelings may be acknowledged, but not submitted to. Reconciliation will require breaking off any romantic affair that may exist. Bill might say to Martha, "Yes, I have developed some very positive feelings for someone else. I will find it very difficult to say no to those feelings, but I will if you are willing to help me restore our marriage."

If, on the other hand, Bill's relationships with other women are simply friendships without romantic feelings or behavior, then he must communicate that clearly to Martha. If Martha finds that hard to believe, he must understand her difficulty. He might say, "Martha, I can understand how you might find it hard to believe what I am saying. I will simply try to demonstrate by my actions that I am not involved with anyone else. I know the day will come when you can believe me again." With those attitudes and actions, Bill demonstrates his seriousness about his efforts at reconciliation. Those efforts should include

21

movement away from female companionship outside the marriage.

Once a couple agrees to work on restoring their marriage they are ready to solve the conflicts that drove them apart. Now they can work on the problem, not on each other.

The "Other Person"

What about the "other woman" or "other man"? Many separations have been precipitated because there was someone else involved. The marital relationship has not been wholesome for many weeks. There is no warmth, understanding, or togetherness. In time, one partner meets someone else and falls in love or at least has a strong physical-emotional attraction that leads to some sort of an affair. At some point, the individual decides to separate, perhaps with the idea that somewhere down the road that new affair might lead to marriage. At any rate, he/she chooses the affair over the present marriage and leaves.

The husband or wife may or may not be aware of the other relationship. In some cases, the spouse will speak openly of the other person, and in others the spouse is extremely secretive. In either case, such activity is counterproductive to reconciliation. An affair with someone else, contrary to what we were told a few years ago by certain psychologists, does not enhance a marriage but destroys it. Research has made that abundantly clear.[1] The Bible has always condemned such behavior as sin (Exodus 20:14). A romantic or sexual relationship with someone else is not the road to reconciliation. It is the sure road to divorce.

Do not misunderstand. I am deeply sympathetic with the dilemma an affair presents. You do not like the idea of divorce, but the affair is so much more meaningful than your marriage. In just a few weeks or months you have come to love this person more than you love your mate. You are able to communicate with such freedom and understanding. It seems that you were meant for each other. How could it be wrong when it seems so right? You know that it is a violation of your marriage vows. You know that such activity is condemned in Scripture. Yet, you reason, God will forgive and in time everything will work out all right.

It is true that God will forgive if we genuinely confess and repent of our sin. Repentance, however, means to *turn from* sin. God will not forgive while we continue to sin. Nor does forgiveness remove all the results of sin. An incident in the life of David is a good example (2 Samuel 11:1—12:31). One morning while doing his exercises, he saw Bathsheba as she bathed herself on a rooftop. He liked what he saw, so he took steps to get a closer look. He brought her to the palace and eventually had sexual relations with her. Having sent her back home, he went about business as usual. Perhaps he did not intend to get further involved, or maybe he would see her only on "special occasions." At any rate, as long as no one knew, it could not hurt.

One small problem developed, however. Bathsheba sent word that she was pregnant. Her husband, Uriah, had been at war for months, so David ordered him home for rest and relaxation, hoping that he would make love with his wife and think the child was his. (Once we have sinned, we begin the process of covering up.) David's plan did not work because Uriah was more loyal to the military than David had imagined. He refused to go home to his wife while his brothers were in battle. David got him drunk, but Uriah's loyalty was stronger than the power of intoxication. Therefore, David moved to plan *B*. He ordered Uriah to the front line, which assured his death. David was free to marry Bathsheba, which he did with haste. Now everything was fine, and they lived happily ever after. Right? Wrong! Read Psalm 51 if you want to hear the confession of a broken heart.

We are never better for having sinned. Confession and forgiveness never remove the negative fall-out of our wrong actions. The emotional scars that come from separation and divorce are never removed. The hurt that is indelibly printed in the minds of children will never be erased. Our whole society has been deeply infected with the "throw-away neurosis." When you are no longer excited about it, get rid of it. It does not matter whether it is a car or a spouse. No wonder our children are so insecure. No wonder there is so little trust in marriage. One's word seems to hold no security.

I am sympathetic with the struggle and pain of losing the warm emotional feelings for one's mate and falling in love with someone else. But we cannot yield to our emotions. All of life is at stake. To follow one's emotions is the surest road to loneliness and ruin. More than half of those who marry new lovers will eventually divorce again. Our best interests are served by returning to our spouses, resolving our conflicts, learning to love, and rediscovering our dreams.

How does one break off an affair? With dignity, respect, kindness, and firmness. You need to indicate to the other person your concern for him or her. You need to confess your wrong in violating your marriage commitment. You need to firmly state your decision to work on reconciliation with your spouse. It is fine to share again your feelings for him or her, but affirm your choice to do what is right rather than what feels good. "Righteousness exalts a nation, but sin is a disgrace to any people" (Proverbs 14:34). What is true on the national level is also true on the personal level. We must not allow our feelings (romantic or otherwise) to determine our destiny. The surest road to failure in life is to follow your feelings. Your greatest happiness is in doing what is right, not in following your emotions.

I am not suggesting that the road to reconciliation is easy, but rather that it is right and that the results are worth the effort.

What if you are the one left at home? Your spouse is having an affair and is now separated from you. Or, you may *think* he or she is having an affair and that that is the reason for separation. First of all, the third person is never the full reason for separation. Almost always there has been some failure in the marriage over a period of time before such an affair develops. The affair may have stimulated the separation, but it did not destroy the marriage. Your failures and those of your spouse brought about the demise of your marriage. Unresolved conflict, unmet needs, and stubborn selfishness eat away at a relationship over the weeks and months.

How shall you respond to your mate's affair? With displeasure, of course. But how will you express your displeasure? With angry outbursts of hate and condemnation? With depression, withdrawal, and suicidal threats? By going out and having an affair yourself? You are disappointed, frustrated, and deeply hurt, but what will lead to reconciliation? None of the above. Yes, you need to express your feelings, but do not play servant to them. Tell your mate how deeply you are hurt, acknowledge your past failures, and ask for reconciliation.

Your spouse may not respond immediately, or the initial response may be hostile, but you have taken the first step. Second, refuse to let the affair be the issue, and resist the temptation to talk about it every time you get together. Concentrate on restoring your own relationship. Your spouse may not break off the affair immediately, but the more you can do to resolve conflicts and communicate hope, the more attractive reconciliation becomes. When you are lashing out in anger or falling apart in self-pity, you do not make reconciliation very desirable.

Express hope and confidence that the two of you can find answers to your past failures. Your hope will tend to stimulate hope in your spouse. Do not demand any particular action. Allow time for your spouse to think, pray, and decide for himself or herself. You cannot force reconciliation—you can only make the prospects look bright. In chapter 5 we shall discuss practical ideas on things you might do.

DATING WHILE SEPARATED

"Should I date while I am separated?" How many times have I heard that question? And, how many times have I given a hard answer? "If you are not free to marry, you are not free to date!" I first read that statement in Britton Wood's book, *Singles Want to Be the Church, Too.*[2] Mr. Wood has worked with singles and separated persons longer than anyone in his denomination. After several years of counseling the separated, I am more convinced than ever that Britton Wood is right. When you start dating someone else while you are separated, you make reconciliation more difficult. The more you date, the muddier the water becomes.

I know that you have needs; you are lonely. Sometimes the load seems unbearable. I know that dating while separated is accepted, even encouraged, in our society. But most of those who are dating will never be reconciled. They will be divorced. Dating is a prelude to remarriage, not therapy for reconciliation. Certainly you need friends. You need a listening ear. You need people who will care and help bear the load, but the dating context is not the best place to find such help. More about where that help can be found is in chapter 4.

You are extremely vulnerable during these days of separation. Unfortunately there are those of the opposite sex who would like to take advantage of your vulnerability. Although pretending to be concerned about you, they are busy satisfying their own desires. I have seen many men and women devastated by such an experience. Your own emotions are erratic, and it would be easy for you to get infatuated with anyone who treats you with dignity, respect, and warmth.

Have you noticed the number of people who get married the day after they are divorced? Obviously they have been dating during separation. If the separation period is a time to seek reconciliation, why spend energy in an activity that leads to divorce and remarriage? Separation is not tantamount to divorce. We are still married while we are separated, and we ought to so live, whether or not our spouse complies.

I know this is difficult to accept, but I believe the present trend of open dating immediately after separation must be deterred. Such activity encourages and contributes to the increasing divorce rate. If you believe in the power of human choice, then you must concede that your estranged spouse may well turn from his or her estrangement and seek reconciliation. You want to be prepared for that day if it comes. Dating someone else is not the way to be prepared. Develop friends, but refuse romantic involvement until the fate of your marriage is determined.

"Shall we draw up separation papers, or does that make divorce more likely?" Many individuals feel that if they sign legal separation papers somehow that means that divorce is inevitable. Such is not the case. Many couples have experienced the joy of burning separation papers in celebration of reconciliation.

Separation papers, in states where they exist, are simply statements upon which both individuals agree that will guide certain aspects of their relationship while they are separated. The two biggest areas of concern are financial and parental. The questions are: How will we handle finances while separated? and, What relationship will each of us have with the children?

If a couple can move toward reconciliation within the first few weeks of separation, then separation papers are unnecessary. That is ideal. Why go to the expense of such legal work if you are going to get together and solve your problems? While you are physically apart, however, you need to mutually agree on some financial arrangement, and discuss your relationship with your children if you are parents. If that cannot be mutually agreed upon, it may indicate that one or both of you are not working at reconciliation.

If after several weeks a couple is not moving toward reconciliation, then legal papers of separation may be in order. That is particularly true when the couple has been unable to reach an equitable financial arrangement and when children are being neglected or abused. In such cases, legal pressure may be necessary to force a spouse to be responsible.

Again, separation papers do not necessarily spell divorce, although in some states they are required before a divorce can be obtained. Separation papers do not determine divorce. What you do and say to each other during the separation period will determine that. Such papers can be destroyed at any point

27

when the two of you are reconciled to life together instead of apart.

Separation is not the time for one spouse to walk on the other. And love must not give license to an irresponsible spouse. An individual who will not meet his or her responsibilities needs someone to hold him accountable. That may have caused part of the problem within the marriage. It must not be allowed to continue during separation. Legal pressure may be of help at this point. Legal papers do not mean that you cannot then be reconciled. If your spouse insists on signing legal papers, little is gained by resisting. You should simply make sure that you can live with the agreements you are signing.

Do not underestimate the matters we have discussed in this chapter. If you are going to work on reconciliation, it is essential that you choose a positive attitude, refuse to foster an extramarital affair, forgo dating, do not blame marital difficulty on someone outside the marriage, and treat each other with dignity and respect during the separation period. To violate those principles is to diminish the hope of reconciliation.

Complete the following assignments with anticipation of understanding yourself and taking constructive steps toward reconciliation.

Growth Assignments

1. Which of your attitudes or actions will have to be changed if you are going to work on reconciliation? Make a list of five statements, each beginning "I will have to . . ."
2. Are you willing to make those changes? If so, why not start today? You need not announce to your spouse what you are doing—simply do it as you have opportunity.

Notes

1. Evelyn Millis Duvall, *Why Wait Till Marriage?* (New York: Association, 1967), pp. 87-88.
   Pitirim Sorokin, *The American Sex Revolution* (Boston: Porter Sargent, 1965), p. 115.
2. Britton Wood, *Single Adults Want to Be the Church, Too* (Nashville: Broadman, 1977), p. 82.

3

Self-Development During Separation

We have said that there are three primary reasons marriages fail: (1) lack of an intimate relationship with God, (2) lack of an intimate relationship with your mate, or (3) lack of an intimate understanding and acceptance of yourself. It is the last of those that we shall explore in this chapter. One might think we would begin with our relationship to God, but the fact is, one's relationship with God is greatly affected by one's self-understanding. Separation should be used as a time to rediscover your own assets and liabilities as a person and to take positive steps in personal growth.

Most of us tend to either underestimate or overestimate our value. We perceive ourselves as either useless failures or as God's gift to the world. Both of those extremes are incorrect. The truth is that your pattern of feeling, thinking, and behaving, which is your *personality,* has both strong and weak points.

INFERIORITY FEELINGS

The person who feels inferior is emphasizing his weak points. If we focus on our failures, we appear to ourselves as failures. If we give attention to our weaknesses, we conceive of ourselves

29

as weak. Inferiority often stems from a childhood in which parents or others have unintentionally communicated that we are dumb, stupid, ugly, clumsy, or not good enough in other ways.

A thirteen-year-old boy suffering from stomach ulcers once told me, "Dr. Chapman, I never do anything right."

"Why do you say that?" I asked.

"Well," he replied, "when I get a *B* on my report card my father always says, 'You should have made an *A*. Son, you're smarter than that.' When I'm playing baseball, if I get a double, my father says, 'You should have made a triple out of that. Can't you run?' When I mow the grass, he says, 'You didn't get under the bushes.' I don't ever do anything right!"

That father had no idea what he was communicating to his son. His objective was to challenge his son to do his best, but in fact, he was communicating to the son that he was inferior.

Usually feelings of inferiority are fed by constant comparison with others. The person who feels inferior will always compare himself with those who are better than he. Of course, everyone can find someone more beautiful or handsome, more athletic, more intelligent. But what about the thousands who rank below you in those areas? The person who feels inferior will never choose to compare himself with those.

I am reminded of the account recorded in Numbers 13. Moses sent out twelve spies into the land of Canaan. The majority report (ten of the twelve) came back: "We saw . . . giants and we were in our own sight as grasshoppers, and so we were in their sight" (v. 33, KJV*). Not only did they see themselves as grasshoppers, but they concluded that others also saw them as weaklings.

That "grasshopper mentality" is typical of those who feel inferior. Scores of women have said, "I feel so ugly, and I know that others think so too." One lady felt so ugly that she refused to go shopping because she did not want to be seen. Without exception those women were *not* ugly. They simply concluded

King James Version.

that others perceived them in the same way that they perceived themselves. Such is rarely true.

Three perspectives go into any self-concept: (1) the way that I see myself, (2) the way that others see me, (3) the way that I think others see me. Numbers 1 and 3 are often identical, but number 2 is almost always different. People simply do not see us as we see ourselves. The person with inferiority feelings can be assured that 99 percent of the people who know him perceive him to be smarter, more attractive, and of greater value than he sees himself. Why live under the illusion that people think you are dumb, ugly, and useless when in fact that is not the way people perceive you?

"But Dr. Chapman," someone will say, "you don't understand. People really do think I'm dumb." Then the person lists all the things that have happened since he was three years old that prove people think he is stupid. I can call in scores of people who can testify to the intelligence of the counselee, but that does not impress him. His mind is made up. He is dumb, and no one is going to convince him otherwise.

No two people are alike. Therefore there are scores of people who have greater abilities than you in particular areas. Others cannot do nearly as well as you can in those same areas. In some tasks you excel. In others you have very little, if any, ability. That is true for all of us. Why should you exalt your weaknesses?

I remember hearing a story when I was a boy that has often come back to encourage me. It seems that a superoptimistic fellow in town made it a practice to attend all funerals and arise at the proper time to say a good word about the departed. In time, the town drunk died. His life had been disgusting in every way. He had been involved in all sorts of criminal activity, had miserably failed his wife and children, had a despicable vocabulary, and had been generally obnoxious all his life. The community gathered to see what the optimist would say now that the end had come.

At the appointed moment, he arose and said one sentence: "He was a good whistler!"

31

Afterward the crowd came to the optimist and one by one said, "I never heard him whistle. Was he a whistler? Did he whistle often?"

The optimist replied, "I only heard him whistle once, but it was good!"

Too bad the drunk had not spent more of his life whistling! If it was the one thing he could do well, what a difference it might have made. What can you do well? Why not concentrate on your *abilities* rather than your inabilities?

After separation, an inferior-feeling person will typically blame himself for the failure of the marriage. Then he or she pleads with the spouse for a chance to start over. When that is spurned, he or she sinks into deep depression and entertains thoughts of suicide. Those people allow the weakest part of their personalties (their feelings of inferiority) to control their behavior.

What is the answer to that downward spiral? One of the most powerful words in the Bible is the admonition of Psalm 15:2, which challenges us to speak the truth in our hearts. We are to tell ourselves the truth. Jesus said the truth liberates us (John 8:31-32).

What is the truth about you? You are made in the image of God. You have tremendous value. Your abilities are many. You have scores of characteristics that others admire. Certainly you have experienced failure. Who hasn't? But that does not mean that you are a failure. You will be a failure only if you choose to fail. On the other hand, if you choose to succeed, nothing, including your feeling of inferiority, can keep you from your goal.

One of the first steps in turning your thinking around is to realize that God has not given up on you. The apostle Paul wrote, "For I am confident of this very thing, that He who began a good work in you will perfect it until the day of Christ Jesus" (Philippians 1:6). In spite of all that has happened, in spite of all your failures, God still intends to bring you to wholeness. He has some strong and positive purposes for your life. You must tell yourself the truth and behave accordingly.

32

The opposite personality type is the individual who feels that he or she is the greatest. He can do no wrong. If there is a problem in the marriage, it is obviously on the part of the spouse. When confronted with his own failure, this kind of personality will admit in a philosophical way that he is not perfect, but insists that the real problem lies with his mate.

This pattern of thinking, feeling, and behaving also begins in childhood. This is the spoiled child. Very few responsibilities were enforced. The child grew up feeling that the world owed him a living. He became demanding of others. Impatient with others' imperfections, he often leaves a trail of broken relationships because he has taken advantage of people. He is very domineering and strong-willed. When he meets resistance from his mate he attempts to force his spouse into line. When the spouse does not shape up, a person who feels superior may choose to separate, placing the blame on the spouse.

What truth will liberate the person with superiority feelings? It is an awareness that the ground is level at the foot of the cross of Christ. We all stand in need of forgiveness. You have failed as well as others. But you have been unwilling to admit your failures, although proclaiming loudly the failure of others. You are important, yes, but no more important than anyone else, including your spouse. You are intelligent, but intelligence is a gift of God for which you should be grateful. You have succeeded in reaching many of your goals. Great! Now learn to share the secret of your success with others and experience the meaning of Jesus' words, "It is more blessed to give than to receive" (Acts 20:35).

Have your feelings of superiority led you to conclude that you are superior? Then it is time for confession and repentance. Come down from your pedestal and enjoy life with the rest of your brothers and sisters. You do not have to claim perfection in order to be important. People will think no less of you if you admit your weaknesses. In fact, your spirit of superiority has driven people away from you in the past.

After separation, the typical person with feelings of superiority will blame the spouse for the breakdown. Even if Mr. or Mrs. Superiority is the one who walked out or got involved in an affair, he or she will almost always blame the spouse for driving him to such action. If the spouse happens to have feelings of inferiority, he will probably accept the blame and suffer accordingly.

People with superiority feelings are quick to rationalize their sinful behavior. They know what the Bible says, *but* . . . They can give you a dozen reasons why in their case it is permissible.

The first step to recovery for the "I am superior" personality is to realize that you are human. No one is perfect. Locate your failures and admit them to God and to your spouse. Be as specific as you can. On the road to confession you will find many friends. The road to self-righteousness gets lonelier each day.

UNDERSTANDING PERSONALITY

We have looked at only one aspect of personality: that of inferior or superior attitudes toward oneself. Personality, however, covers the entire spectrum of human experience. When I use the word *personality*, I am speaking of your own unique pattern of thinking, feeling, and behaving. No two personalities are alike, although in certain aspects of personality people tend to fit into general categories. Most traits are expressed by contrasting words. We speak of an individual's being optimistic or pessimistic, negative or positive, critical or complimentary, extroverted or introverted, talkative or quiet, patient or impatient.

Our personalities greatly influence the way we live. The tragedy of our day is that we have been led to believe that our personalities are set in concrete by age five or six, and that our destinies are determined. Many feel trapped. They look at the thought, feeling, and behavior patterns that have caused them problems in the past and conclude that nothing can be done to change those patterns. But nothing could be further from the truth.

34

It is true that as adults, those tendencies may persist. That is, we are influenced by certain personality patterns. Our lives, however, do not have to be governed by those patterns. The whole idea of education, spiritual conversion, and Christian growth stands in opposition to the idea of determinism, the idea that our quality of life is determined by patterns established in childhood. The message of the Bible is that we are responsible for the quality of life we live. Our response to God, our conscious decisions, our choice of attitudes will determine that quality. We must not see ourselves enslaved by our personalities. We need to understand our personality patterns, to utilize our strengths for good, and to seek growth in the areas of weakness. Excel in your strengths and grow in your weaknesses.

What do you know about yourself? What kind of person have you been through the years? Has your spirit been negative or positive toward life? One wife said, "My husband is so negative that when he wakes up in the morning he either says, 'Oh, no, I overslept!' or, 'Oh, no, I woke up too early!'" For that husband, every day started off wrong. With that attitude there is no way to win. That may appear foolish as you read it, but thousands of people choose to live life with just that attitude. Something is always wrong with everything. Could that be your attitude? If so, do you think it contributed to the breakdown of your marriage? Can you imagine the emotional drain on your spouse when he/she hears your daily newscast of doom?

Are you critical or complimentary toward others? Toward yourself? Look back over this day. Have you given yourself a compliment? Have you complimented anyone else? On the other hand, have you made a critical statement about someone? About yourself? Has that been a pattern of life for you? How has that affected your marriage?

What have been your patterns of communication? Do you tend to hold things inside or to let it out? One wife reported, "My husband did not share with me what was going on in his life. He basically lived his life, and I lived mine. I did not like

35

it, but I did not know what to do about it. One day he came home and told me that he was leaving. I couldn't believe it. I had no idea that it was that bad."

How could such a situation arise? One or both partners yielded to a natural tendency to keep it all inside and slowly but surely put their marriage to sleep. Can such a marriage be healed? Yes, but it will likely require surgery (the skill of a counselor or pastor). Once our feelings are expressed we can seek solutions. No one, including your spouse, can work on a solution until he is aware of the problem.

Do you keep your feelings bottled up inside? Then use this time of separation to learn to release those feelings. Find a counselor or trusted friend and ask for help. When you learn to communicate constructively with someone else, you can then communicate with your spouse. The tendency to keep quiet is not all bad. The Scriptures even challenge us to be "slow to speak" (James 1:19). It is when that tendency is carried to the extreme that it causes problems. As you discover your basic personality weaknesses, you will likely see how they have affected your marriage. *Those patterns can be changed significantly with the help of God.*

Accepting the Unchangeable

"Can the Ethiopian change his skin or the leopard his spots?" (Jeremiah 13:23). Jesus asked, "Which of you by being anxious can add a single cubit to his life's span?" (Matthew 6:27). Some things cannot be changed. Your height, skin color, hair texture and amount, and color of eyes are pretty well settled unless modern medical science comes up with some new discoveries.

Perhaps the most influential unchangeable factor is your history. By definition, it cannot be changed. It is past. The past cannot be relived. Your parents, for better or worse, dead or alive, known or unknown, are your parents. That fact cannot be changed. Your childhood, pleasant or painful, is your childhood and stands as history.

Your marriage or marriages fall into the same category. It is

36

futile to reason, "We should never have gotten married in the first place." The fact cannot be changed. The events that have transpired in your marriage are also history. You can undo none of them. No words can be retracted, no deed recalled. We can ask forgiveness for failures, but even that does not remove all of the effects of our sin.

Our history is not to be changed, but accepted. When Jesus met the woman at the well, He did not ask that she erase her five marriages, for such would have been impossible; He simply offered her water that would quench her obvious thirst (John 4:5-29).

We waste our time and energy when we ponder what might have been: "If I had" or "if he/she had. . . ." We must simply admit failure to ourselves, God, and our spouses. Accept God's forgiveness, forgive yourself, and trust that your spouse will do the same. Beyond that, you cannot deal with the past. You must concentrate on the future, for it is in your hands to shape.

Why not use some time while separated to take an honest look at your personality? Discover your basic patterns of thought, feeling, and behavior. Then decide where your strengths lie and utilize them to expand your horizons. At the same time be realistic about your weaknesses. Decide what needs to be changed and take steps toward growth. Admit those things that cannot be changed and accept them. This could be an exciting time of self-discovery and growth for you. You can be a different person in a few months.

DISCOVERING GROWTH POSSIBILITIES

Not only is separation a time to examine the strengths and weaknesses of your personality, it is also a time to develop your creative abilities. Unless you have children, separation gives you more free time than when you were living with your spouse. Why not use some of that time to develop latent interests you have neglected? Read those books you have intended to read. Take piano or guitar lessons. Enroll in your local college or technical institute to prepare for a vocation or simply to develop new friends. Attend concerts and dramas. Learn to play tennis. Most communities offer hundreds of opportunities for development of interests and abilities.

I know that in the pain of separation you may not feel like undertaking any of the above. Perhaps you have lost your interest in the midst of your loneliness and hurt. Sitting at home reflecting on your problems, however, will only lead to deeper depression. Once you take a step to develop an old interest the sun may break through the darkness.

Concentrate on small, attainable goals at first. Do not look at the rest of your life as one great unknown. Make plans for today. What can you do today that will be constructive? As you fill your days with meaningful activity, hope for the future will grow.

As you come to understand yourself, develop yourself, accept yourself, you enhance the prospects of reconciliation with your spouse.

Growth Assignments

1. You may want to ask a pastor or counselor to arrange for you to take the Taylor-Johnson Temperament Analysis or the Myers-Briggs Personality Inventory. Either will help you identify personality patterns.
2. You may want to read *You Can Change Your Personality* by Andre Bustanoby. (See Appendix.)
3. You may want to enroll in a class on personality development at your church or community college.
4. Try the following to get started:

UNDERSTANDING AND ACCEPTING MYSELF

Write your answers to the following questions:
1. What do I like about myself?
2. What emotions do I feel today? Divide those into two columns: Negative feelings   Positive feelings
3. What do my negative feelings tell me about myself?
4. What do my positive feelings tell me about myself?
5. What are my emotional needs today?

38

6. How can I meet those needs in a responsible Christian way?
7. What would I like to see changed in my personality (i.e., my way of thinking, feeling, and behaving)?
8. What step will I take today to effect that change?
9. What do I dislike about myself but cannot change?
10. Will you accept that characteristic and concentrate on your assets? _____Yes _____No

4

Developing Your Relationship
with God

PSALM 77:1-15

My voice rises to God, and I will cry aloud;
My voice rises to God, and He will hear me.
In the day of my trouble I sought the Lord;
In the night my hand was stretched out without weariness;
My soul refused to be comforted.
When I remember God, then I am disturbed;
When I sigh, then my spirit grows faint.

Thou hast held my eyelids open;
I am so troubled that I cannot speak.
I have considered the days of old,
The years of long ago.
I will remember my song in the night;
I will meditate with my heart;
And my spirit ponders.

Will the Lord reject forever?
And will He never be favorable again?
Has His lovingkindness ceased forever?
Has His promise come to an end forever?
Has God forgotten to be gracious?
Or has He in anger withdrawn His compassion?
Then I said, "It is my grief,
That the right hand of the Most High has changed."

I shall remember the deeds of the LORD;
Surely I will remember Thy wonders of old.
I will meditate on all Thy work,
And muse on Thy deeds.
Thy way, O God, is holy;
What god is great like our God?
Thou art the God who workest wonders;
Thou hast made known Thy strength among the peoples.
Thou hast by Thy power redeemed Thy people,
The sons of Jacob and Joseph.

Our relationships with God may make or break our marriages. Augustine said, "Man was made by God and does not find rest until he finds God." If we look to a marriage partner to give us a sense of worth and to bring happiness, we are looking in the wrong direction. Many have expected a spouse to provide that which only God can give. Peace of mind, inner security, a confidence in the outcome of life, and a sense of joy about living do not come from marriage, but from an intimate relationship with God.

What has been your relationship with God during the time you have been separated? Many individuals find themselves angry with God; angry because God has allowed the pain, the loneliness, and the frustration that comes with a broken marital relationship. Others have found themselves turning to God in a fresh and deep way to seek God's help.

Psalm 77 is a personal expression of one individual who was going through a time of great crisis. You will note that there is first a description of the pain of being estranged from God and from others. But out of the midst of that pain the psalmist turns to God and remembers more pleasant days when he knew the blessing of God and wholesome relationships with others in his life.

The passage ends with a very graphic description of his present state: "Thou hast by Thy power redeemed Thy people" (v. 15). The word *redeem* means to "buy back" or "restore." That is always God's desire for His people. The process, however, may be painful. David said, "Thy way was in the sea, and Thy paths in the mighty waters, and Thy footprints may not be known" (Psalm 77:19). You may feel that you are indeed walking through the sea in the midst of mighty waters and that you cannot see the footprints of God. But I assure you, God *is* vitally concerned about you and your present state. The words of Jesus, "Come to Me, all who are weary and heavy-laden, and I will give you rest" (Matthew 11:28), are directed to you as surely as they were directed to those to whom Jesus spoke. Yes, you are weary from much stress. You are heavy-laden, burdened perhaps with guilt, anger, hostility, and anxiety. You will notice that Jesus does not ask that you lay the burden aside and come to Him, but rather that you just come. He has promised to give rest. He has not asked you to handle your own problems, nor has He promised to take away the problems, but He has promised rest.

God is your friend, if not your Father. The Scriptures teach He is the Father of all those who come to Him through Jesus Christ His Son. He is not the Father of all—only of those who acknowledge Jesus Christ as Lord. But He is the friend of all. It is God's desire to share life with us, to help us find meaning and purpose in life, to give us answers to the problems we encounter. In the midst of our pain it is sometimes difficult to believe that God could do anything for us. May I suggest steps that will help you in personal spiritual growth during these days of separation?

DEAL WITH FAILURE

It may be true as you analyze your marriage that you discern your own role in that failure. On the other hand, it may be that you see more clearly the failures of your spouse, and you have spent many hours in accusing him/her of those failures. If Jesus' words in Matthew 7 were applied to marriage, they would read: "Why do you behold the speck that is in your mate's eye, when, behold, there is a beam in your own eye? First pull the beam out of your own eye, then you can see more clearly how to get the speck out of your mate's eye" (Matthew 7:3-5).

Our natural tendency is to seek to place blame with our mates and to reason in our hearts that if our mates would

43

change, our marriages would be restored. Jesus said, however, that we must begin with our own sins. Whether that sin is large or small, it is the only sin that we can confess. If we confess our own failures, we will be better equipped to help with the failures of our spouses. When we fail our marriage partners, we also fail God, for Jesus admonished us to love one another (John 13:34). The only true way to express our love for God is by expressing our love for each other. When we fail to love each other, we have failed in our love for God. Therefore, we must confess the failures of the marriage to God.

Perhaps the most powerful verse in the Bible on mental health is Acts 24:16, where Paul says about himself, "I [discipline myself] to maintain always a blameless conscience both before God and before men." Paul spoke from personal experience. He had learned that it takes discipline to deal with one's failure, but that discipline is necessary if we are to be emotionally, spiritually free. Thus, Paul said, "I empty my conscience toward God and toward men." The process of emptying our conscience is confession. The word *confession* literally means "to agree with." Thus we agree with God about our failures. No longer are we excusing ourselves and our behavior, but we are acknowledging before God that we have sinned. The Scriptures teach believers that when we confess our sins God "is faithful and righteous to forgive us our sins and to cleanse us from all unrighteousness" (1 John 1:9). The moment we are willing to acknowledge our failure, God is willing to forgive our sin. But as long as we excuse our sin, God will not hear our prayers (Psalm 66:18).

The first step, then, in developing your relationship with God is to confess all known sin. I suggest that you take pencil and paper and say to God, "Lord, where have I failed in my marriage?" As God brings truth to your mind, write it down and make a list of your failures. Then go over your list, confessing each sin, thanking God that Christ has paid the penalty for your sin, and accepting His forgiveness for that sin. The experience of forgiveness liberates us from the guilt that burdens us. Without confession, there can be no forgiveness. Without forgiveness, we are in bondage to guilt.

Confession and forgiveness do not mean that we will immediately lose all remorseful feelings about our sin. Forgiveness is God's promise that He will no longer hold our sin against us. We may still feel horrible when we reflect upon what we have done or failed to do, but our feelings have nothing to do with God's forgiveness. We must not allow those feelings to defeat us. When feelings of guilt return after confession, we simply say, "Thank You, Father, that those sins are forgiven and that You no longer hold them against me. Help me to forgive myself." Forgiving yourself is also a promise. You promise yourself that you will no longer punish yourself for past failures. Such punishment produces nothing positive, but keeps you from making the most of your future.

When we confess our sin to God, it is as though we have come home from a long journey and our father welcomes us with extended arms, forgives our sin, "kills the fatted calf," and makes a feast to celebrate our return (Luke 15:21-24). Such a return to God may be the most significant thing that happens while you are separated, for you are now returning to the One who made you and knows how to lead you in productive living.

LEARN TO COMMUNICATE

Your relationship with God will grow only if you learn to communicate with Him. I must remind you that communication is a two-way process. Not only do we talk to God, but God talks to us. Many people are familiar with prayer, whereby we talk to God, but few people hear the voice of God. I am not suggesting that God speaks in an audible voice to us. But through the Bible God speaks in a very personal way to those who will take the time to listen.

Some think of reading the Bible and praying as simply religious activities, but they are meant to be avenues of intimate fellowship between an individual and God. As we read the Bible, God will speak to us about Himself and about our lives.

45

The Bible is more relevant than any book you will ever read on human relationships, for it is indeed the God of creation speaking to His creature. Here are some practical ideas on communicating with God: Since the Bible is God's Word to us, one ought to read it with a listening ear, an ear open to hear His voice. When we read other books, we are careful to underline the important ideas in each chapter. Why not do the same with the Bible? As you read the Scriptures, certain phrases, sentences, and ideas will stand out in each chapter. It is likely that those are the ideas God seeks to communicate to you. Why not underline, circle, or put a star by them to draw your attention to those ideas?

For many years I have followed the practice of daily sitting down with God, opening the Bible, and beginning the conversation with these words: "Father, this is Your day in my life. I want to hear Your voice. I need Your instructions. I want to know what You would say to me this day. As I read this chapter, bring to my mind the things You want me to hear." Then I read the chapter silently or aloud with pen in hand, marking those things that stand out as I read. Sometimes I read the chapter a second time, saying, "Lord, I'm not sure I understood what You were saying; I want to read again. I want You to clarify what's on Your mind for me." I may underline additional lines or phrases.

Having completed the chapter, I then go back and talk to God about what I've underlined, for if that is what God is saying to me I want to respond to God. Many people simply read the Bible, close it, and then begin praying about something totally unrelated to what they have read. Nothing could be more discourteous. We would not treat a friend like that. If a friend asks a question, we give an answer. If a friend makes a statement, we have a response, so if God speaks to us through the Bible we should respond to what God is saying.

For example, let us say that I am reading from Philippians, chapter 4, and the thing that impresses me is the statement in verse 4, "Rejoice in the Lord always; again I will say, rejoice!" So I underline the sentence, and I circle the word *always*. Then

I go back to God and say, "Lord, how can this be? It seems utterly impossible that I can rejoice *always*. Sometimes, yes, but always?" You see, I'm responding to what God has said to me with a question. I read the sentence again: "Rejoice in the Lord always; again I will say rejoice!" and I see those little words *in the Lord,* and God has answered my question. What He is saying is that I am to rejoice in the *Lord* always, not in circumstances, for I cannot rejoice in adverse circumstances. But I can rejoice in the Lord in the midst of those circumstances. Because of my relationship with Him, I can indeed rejoice in the midst of my present problem. What an encouragement to one who is going through deep waters!

Every day God desires to speak to us in a very personal way from His word, and He desires us to respond. May I challenge you to begin today by reading a chapter each day in the Bible, underlining and marking, and then talking to God about what you have marked? Let me suggest that you begin with one book. (James is a good place to start.) Complete that book before beginning another. You will leave a trail through the Bible where you have walked with God, and you can easily refer back to the things God has said to you day by day and week by week. You will find that your relationship with God is greatly enhanced, for nothing builds relationships like open communication.

Choose to Obey

As you read the Scriptures, you will on occasion find clear commands of God such as "be kind to one another, tender-hearted, forgiving each other, just as God in Christ also has forgiven you" (Ephesians 4:32). Such commands are given for our good. God, who made us, knows precisely what will make us happy and fruitful in life. All of His commands are given with purpose, so we must choose in our own hearts to obey every command we hear from God. Thus, if we read "be kind to one another," we ought to seek someone to whom we can be kind that day—someone to whom we can be tender-hearted, someone whom we can forgive, even if he is not asking forgive-

47

ness. Our example is Christ, who forgave us. You will remember on the cross Christ looked on those who were crucifying Him and said, "Father, forgive them; for they do not know what they are doing" (Luke 23:34). Is that not what we need to do for others? It is the clear teaching of the Bible. There are literally hundreds of commands in Scripture that will greatly enhance our lives as we respond in obedience.

We are not left to depend on our own power when it comes to obedience, for if we are Christians we have within us the Holy Spirit, who gives us the power to obey the commands of God. So if you find it difficult to forgive those who have sinned against you, there is help. Do not simply try in your own power to forgive, but ask the Spirit of God to enable you to forgive. Forgiveness is basically a promise. It is a promise that we will no longer hold a person's failures against him. It does not mean we are unaware of those failures, but it means we will not treat them as failures. It does not mean, in the strictest sense, that we will forget the sins, insofar as being aware they have been committed is concerned. But we are able, with God's help, to no longer hold the sin of another against him.

Can you envision what might happen in your life if you would begin reading the Scriptures daily, listening to the voice of God, and responding to His commands, in the power of the Holy Spirit? It is conceivable that in a few months you will hardly recognize yourself, for tremendous changes will take place day by day.

SING TO THE LORD

Music is a universal expression of human feeling. If you listen to the songs of cultures around the world you will find the themes of joy, excitement, and thrill; but you will also find the themes of sorrow, pain, and hurt. That is true in both religious and secular music. Singing is a vehicle of communication. It can lift the heart or depress the spirit. The words of our songs determine whether they will lead us to depression or lead us to victory. Throughout the Psalms we are challenged to sing praise to the Lord. In the midst of pain, we may wonder,

48

"For what can I praise God?" As we reflect upon the truth, however, we will find many things for which we can praise God.

In the psalm mentioned above, David praised God for His past benefits, His past blessings. As we begin to praise God for what He has done in the past, we come to thank God that He will be faithful to us in the future. Paul wrote to the Ephesians that they were to be filled or controlled with the Holy Spirit, and then they were to speak to one another in "psalms and hymns and spiritual songs, singing and making melody" in their hearts to the Lord (Ephesians 5:18-19). Our songs of joy and triumph must grow out of our relationships with God. As we are controlled by the Spirit of God, we may sing of our problems, but the heart of our music will be praise to God for who He is and what He is doing in our lives.

Our relationships with God are not hindered by our present circumstances; instead, our circumstances may push us to God. You may not be inclined to sing. You may never have sung in your life, but as a Christian you can sing if only in private. In fact, Paul says we are to sing to ourselves. That may be in the shower, it may be in bed. May I suggest if that is not a normal practice in your life that you simply take one of the psalms (remember, that was the hymnbook of the Jew) and make up your own tune and sing that psalm to God. Melody, pitch, and rhythm are unimportant. What is important is that you are expressing praise to God through the words of others who have walked through difficulty. You might begin with Psalm 77, which is printed above.

FIND OTHER CHRISTIANS

You may or may not presently be involved in a local church fellowship. During separation it is particularly important that you find other Christians with whom you can fellowship. It is true that the church can be justly criticized. How often we hear individuals say, "I don't want to attend that church because it's filled with hypocrites." That is likely true. Hypocrites and sinners regularly attend most churches, but without hypocrites and sinners, who would be left to attend? For we have all sinned, and we are all sometimes hypocritical. Attending church does not mean we are perfect. It means that we are seeking growth.

In most Christian churches you are likely to find friendly people who will welcome you and who will seek to help you. We were not meant to live alone. It was God who said in the beginning, "It is not good for the man to be alone" (Genesis 2:18). The psalmist also said, "God makes a home for the lonely" (Psalm 68:6). During these days when you are separated from your spouse you desperately need the fellowship of the larger family of God.

When many people think of church, they think only of attending the Sunday morning worship service. That is fine, but it is only a part of any church worthy of the name. The church is "the called-out ones," those who have responded to Jesus Christ as Lord and who come together to learn and to encourage each other. Small Bible study and prayer groups are vital in the fellowship of a church. Be sure that you do not simply sample the Sunday sermon. Get involved in the small group studies where you can find answers to the questions that arise. Many churches offer classes designed to help the separated. Most pastors are also willing to give personal counseling.

If you have not been attending church regularly, start this Sunday. Find a group of Christians with whom you can identify and with whom you can come to share and who will give you the encouragement and support you need.

You must not come to the church with the idea of receiving only, but you must also come with the idea of giving of your ability to others. You may ask, "What do I have to offer anyone else? I can't handle my own problems." The fact is, you will probably encounter others at the church who have problems similar to yours, and you may be able to share with them something you are discovering in your relationship with God. Attending church is never a one-way street. We are told in Hebrews 10 that we are to exhort, comfort, and encourage each other, and that is likely to take place in any Christian church that is authentic.

Earlier I mentioned the words of Jesus, "Come to Me, all who are weary and heavy-laden, and I will give you rest" (Matthew 11:28). Jesus went on to say, "Take My yoke upon you, and learn from Me, for I am gentle and humble in heart; and YOU SHALL FIND REST FOR YOUR SOULS. For My yoke is easy, and My load is light" (11:29-30). Jesus does not call us to lay down our load in order to find rest. He calls us to take His yoke upon us. The yoke speaks of work. We are challenged not to inactivity, not to simple rest, but we are challenged to take upon ourselves the yoke of Christ and to blend our lives with the lives of other Christians in accomplishing good for God in the world. Jesus says, "My yoke is easy and My load is light." Compared to what? Compared to the yoke and load we bear when we choose to walk our own way. As we walk our own way, giving no thought to God or His Word, we find our yoke is heavy and our load becomes heavier as the days come and go. But as we walk with Christ we find His yoke is easy, His load is light compared to what we have borne before. And His burden is always with purpose. Yes, there is work to be done, but that work is purposeful.

I have known many separated individuals who have spent hours of dedicated service helping the church office or janitorial staff or in reaching out to those who are sick or in trouble. Your own pain does not render you ineffective with others. Indeed, it may equip you to share with others. The road to happiness is not found in isolation, concentrating on one's problems; the road to happiness is found by sharing life with God and learning to serve Him.

GROWTH ASSIGNMENTS

1. If you have not already done so, ask God to bring to your mind the areas in which you have failed in your marriage.
2. Make a list of your failures and confess each one to God. Thank Him that Christ has paid the penalty for those sins, and accept His forgiveness.

51

3. Begin the practice of reading, marking, and talking to God about a chapter in the Bible each day. You may want to begin with the book of James in the New Testament.
4. Try singing a psalm to God. Make your own tune and rhythm. You may begin with Psalm 1.
5. If you are not active in a local church, decide today which church you will visit next Sunday. Be sure to attend the Bible study class as well as the worship service.
6. Don't give up the search until you find a warm, loving, group of Christians with whom you can share life.

5

Developing Your Relationship with Your Mate

"How can I develop a relationship when we are living apart?" is a valid question. Bob and Janice have been separated for three months. The only contact they have had is when they met briefly with a lawyer to discuss the terms of legal separation. Obviously neither Bob nor Janice has had much of an opportunity to develop a relationship with the other. Is there hope for their marriage? Not until someone seeks to penetrate the silence. As long as each stubbornly refuses to talk with the other, reconciliation lies as a wrecked plane on a desert, hopelessly beyond repair.

It only takes one person, however, to break the silence. It takes *both* to communicate, but only one to initiate the process. Have you been standing off, refusing to give in and call, waiting for your spouse to make the first move? Why wait? The responsibility is yours to seek reconciliation (Matthew 5:23-24; 18:15-17). You may not be able to effect reconciliation, but you must seek it.

Sometimes the fixing of blame keeps us from taking the first step. We reason, "He/she failed me. Why should I be the one to reach out?" Let him come to me and ask forgiveness!" That line of reasoning is perfectly normal, but it is not biblical. Jesus said, "If therefore you are presenting your offering at the altar, and there remember that your brother has something against you, leave your offering there before the altar, and go your way; first be reconciled to your brother, and then come and present your offering" (Matthew 5:23-24).

Later Jesus said, "And if your brother sins, go and reprove him in private; if he listens to you, you have won your brother. But if he does not listen to you, take one or two more with you, SO THAT BY THE MOUTH OF TWO OR THREE WITNESSES EVERY FACT MAY BE CONFIRMED. And if he refuses to listen to them, tell it to the church; and if he refuses to listen even to the church, let him be to you as a Gentile and a tax-gatherer" (Matthew 18:15-17).

If those principles apply to the church at large, surely they apply to a Christian couple who are separated. Those passages teach that whether you have sinned against your spouse or your spouse has sinned against you (both are likely true), the responsibility for seeking reconciliation lies with you. With your own sin, you must go admitting wrong and asking forgiveness. For your spouse's sin, you must go willing to forgive if he or she is willing to confess and repent.

THE ART OF CONFESSION

In all of my counseling, I have never seen a couple in which both were not at fault to some degree. One may have committed the overt act of adultery or lived an egocentric life-style with little concern for the needs of the spouse, but the spouse also had failures. It is easy for us to identify the failures of our mates, but more difficult to admit our own. I have often given individuals a sheet of paper and asked them to list the faults of their spouses. They will write profusely for ten or fifteen minutes. Some have even asked for more paper. The lists are magnificent and detailed.

When I ask them to make a list of their own faults they immediately list their one big fault. That is followed with a long period of silence as they try to think of number 2. Some never find it, and seldom has anyone come back with more than four personal faults. What does that tell us? That the spouse really is the problem? Hardly, for each spouse has a grand list of the other's faults. It tells us that we tend to see ourselves through rose-colored glasses. Our faults do not look very big to us because we are used to them. We have lived with them for years. Naturally then, we attribute the real problem to our mate's behavior.

In chapter 4 we noted Jesus' words, "And why do you look at the speck in your brother's eye, but do not notice the log that is in your own eye? Or how can you say to your brother, 'Let me take the speck out of your eye,' and behold, the log is in your own eye? You hypocrite, first take the log out of your own eye; and then you will see clearly to take the speck out of your brother's eye" (Matthew 7:3-5). Note, Jesus did not say that your spouse was perfect. He simply said that the place to begin in improving relationships is with the "log that is in your own eye." When you have identified and confessed your own wrongs you can see more clearly how to help your spouse with his/her faults.

Failures come in two basic areas. First we fail in meeting the needs of our partners, and second we fail by doing and saying things that actually are designed to hurt them. We fail to do what we *should* do for them and end up doing what we *should not* do toward them. Certainly it was not our desire to fail. We had dreams of making our mates supremely happy, but when our own needs were not met, we became cool and later hostile. Paul describes our problem in Romans 7, where he talks about his own experience: "For that which I am doing, I do not understand; for I am not practicing what I would like to do, but I am doing the very thing I hate" (v. 15). He goes on to describe the reason for such behavior. We allow our old, sinful, selfish nature to control our behavior. Our only hope for change, Paul says, is to allow Jesus Christ our Lord to control our lives. He alone can give us the power to actually do what we know is right.

The first step toward restoration is confession to your mate.

One warning: Do not blame yourself for the failure of your marriage. It is not totally your fault, but you are not perfect. You have failed, and Jesus said the place to begin is by confessing your failure to your spouse and asking forgiveness. I would suggest you ask God to help you make a list of your failures. Write them down. Be as specific as possible. Having asked God's forgiveness, ask Him to give you courage to show the list to your spouse.

Admitting your wrong and asking forgiveness will not guarantee the restoration of your marriage, but it will give you a clear conscience (Acts 24:16). You will never be free from guilt until you admit your part in the marital failure. Your spouse may or may not forgive you. He/she may or may not be open to reconciliation. When you have asked forgiveness, however, you have done all that you can do to correct the past. It cannot be erased. It can only be confessed.

Now, what about the sins of your spouse? There can be no genuine reconciliation unless he or she is willing to confess and turn from past failures. That, however, is something one spouse cannot do for another. Your mate must choose to forsake his or her sin and return to you. If he chooses confession and repentance, you must stand ready to forgive and receive. Your spouse cannot undo the past any more than you can. He can turn around and walk away from that sin and seek reconciliation. He may not do that, however, the same day you make your confession. You must be willing to wait, pray, and love, even if at a distance.

THE POWER OF PRAYER

Your prayer must not be: "Lord, if it is Your will bring him/her back." We already know it is God's will for marriages to be restored, however, God respects human freedom. For what should you pray then?

Jesus said about the Holy Spirit, "And He, when He comes, will convict the world concerning sin, and righteousness, and judgment" (John 16:8). I believe that you should pray for the specific work of the Holy Spirit in the life of your spouse. You

56

should pray that God will effect a deep sense of guilt for his or her sin; that He will impart a genuine awareness of what it means to be righteous (right); and an understanding of the reality of judgment to come upon those who do not repent. Such praying is in keeping with what we know to be the work of the Holy Spirit. God will answer that prayer.

How will your spouse respond? Your spouse may choose to respond to the work of the Holy Spirit and turn from sin. On the other hand, he or she may reject all of God's pressure and walk his own way. You must give your mate the same liberty God gives.

Some people blame God for allowing their marriages to break up. Do not feel that God has not answered your prayer if your spouse refuses to return. Individuals choose to get married, choose their behavior patterns toward each other, and choose to separate or resolve problems. If God did not allow such freedom He would have to reduce man to something less than man. He would have to remove the imprint of God's image in man.

Do not give up. It takes time for individuals to respond to God's leading. Continue to pray for your spouse until God's will is perfected in his or her life.

LEARNING TO LOVE

Having confessed your past failures, asked forgiveness, and sought reconciliation, what do you do while waiting? Try love! Loving your spouse while estranged is not the easiest task in the world, but it may be the most productive. Many will balk at the statement *try love!* Our society has defined love as something that happens to you, not something over which you have control. For example, many will say very sincerely, "I just don't love him/her anymore. I wish I could, but too much has happened." The thesis of that statement is that love is an emotion, a warm, bubbly, excited positive feeling one has for a member of the opposite sex. You either have it or you don't. If you don't, there is nothing you can do about it. You must simply move away and hope that you may find it with someone else someday, somewhere.

That concept of love has been one of the greatest contributors to divorce in our generation. It makes marriage hopeless and divorce inevitable if one does not have a certain emotion. Since we have no choice as to our emotions we are pawns to whatever causes our emotions. Thus, man is no longer responsible for his actions. Behavior is explained in terms of "being true to one's feelings." Nothing is right or wrong. Man simply does what he feels like doing. Such a philosophy enslaves man to some great unknown cause behind his emotions.

The biblical concept of love is that it is something we *choose*. It is not an emotion, but an attitude, a way of thinking. Love is the attitude that says, "I will put your best interests as priority in my life." Love will then be accompanied by appropriate behavior. Attitude and action always go together. If we choose to *think* a certain way, then we will behave in a corresponding manner. The Bible commands husbands to love their wives (Ephesians 5:25). Older women are instructed to teach younger wives to love their husbands (Titus 2:3-4). Anything that can be commanded, and anything that can be taught and learned, is not beyond our control.

Love is a choice. You can love your spouse in spite of what he/she has done or failed to do. You can love your spouse in spite of your feelings. You may feel disappointed, hurt, rejected, lonely, angry, frustrated, hostile, and any number of negative emotions and yet choose to love your spouse. We are not slaves to our emotions. That is one of the most liberating truths found in the Bible. It is normal for you to feel negative emotions in light of the way your mate has treated you. It is not Christian, however, to allow those emotions to dominate your thoughts and behavior.

Our best example is Jesus, who loved even those who crucified Him. He prayed from the cross, "Father forgive them; for they do not know what they are doing" (Luke 23:34). But He is not our only example. I could share from my files scores of couples who have chosen the high road of love in spite of negative feelings. I am not suggesting that negative emotions should be repressed or denied. Those feelings must be acknowledged to yourself, God, and your mate. We acknowledge our feelings, but we do not serve them.

One man said to his wife, who had been unfaithful to him sexually, "I am so angry, hurt, disappointed, and crushed. One minute I feel like committing suicide and the next like slapping you in the face, but with the help of God I know there is a better way. I know that I have failed you in many ways. Last night I made a list of some of my failures. I want to share it and ask forgiveness. If you are willing, I would like to work on finding answers to our problems." The man did not deny his feelings, but made a conscious choice of a better way.

We have said that love is the attitude that exalts the interests of the other person. Love says, "I want to do everything in my power to help my mate grow as a person. I want to meet all of his/her needs that lie within my power to meet. I want to help him over emotional or social hang-ups. I want to help him reach all of his potential for God and good in the world."

The characteristics of love are described in 1 Corinthians 13: "Love is patient, love is kind. It does not envy, it does not boast, it is not proud. It is not rude, it is not self-seeking, it is not easily angered, it keeps no record of wrongs. Love does not delight in evil, but rejoices with the truth. It always protects, always trusts, always hopes, always perseveres" (vv. 4-7, NIV).

Love, as it is described in the Bible, does not come naturally. By nature, if your mate is not loving you, then you will not love him or her. Yet Jesus said, "Love your enemies, bless them that curse you, do good to them that hate you, and pray for them which despitefully use you, and persecute you. . . . For if ye love them which love you, what reward have ye?" (Matthew 5:44, 46, KJV). Is your husband your enemy? Does your wife hate you? Jesus' command is to love him or her. Such a command would be impossible to fulfill if love were an emotion. Note the words Jesus used to express love: *do good, bless, pray for*. Those are action words, not descriptions of emotions. Love is expressed by actions designed to help the other individual. The emotional aspect of love will take care of itself if we concentrate on the action aspect.

How can you love your spouse when he or she is not showing love to you? Only with divine help! In Romans 5 we read, "the love of God has been poured out within our hearts through the Holy Spirit who was given to us" (v. 5). Our greatest source of help is God. If you are a Christian, God has given you His Spirit as a constant companion. The Holy Spirit wants to fill our lives with love. If you can see yourself as a channel of God's love to your mate, you will have the biblical picture. God wants to express His love, care, and concern for your spouse. You can be God's chief channel. You must first receive God's forgiveness and invite His Spirit to fill your life with love.

You do not have the same opportunities to love your mate that you had when you were living together. You do, however, have opportunities. The next chapter will explore some of those opportunities, but first complete the following growth assignments.

GROWTH ASSIGNMENTS

1. Ask God to help you make a list of the specific ways in which you have failed your spouse. (You may simply add to the list you made in chapter 4).
2. Confess those to God, if you have not already done so, and accept His forgiveness.
3. Ask God to fill you with His love (Romans 5:5) and to let you be His agent for loving your spouse.
4. Arrange to see your spouse and share your list and ask forgiveness. Share your desire for a chance to work on your problems and find reconciliation, but do not demand that he or she give you an answer immediately.
5. While you wait for his or her response, pray that God will convict him of sin, righteousness, and judgment.
6. Read chapter 6 for practical ideas on how to express love while you are separated.

6

Long Distance Love

Your spouse is no longer coming home at the end of the day. When you walk into your home no one is there to greet you. If you love at all, it must be at a distance and sporadically expressed. Some separated couples have a great deal of contact, whereas others see each other seldom if ever. Thus, some of you will have more opportunity to express love to your spouses than others. Do not decry your circumstance. Your situation is your situation, and you must make the most of it. Using the descriptive words of 1 Corinthians 13, I want to suggest some practical ways of expressing love while separated.

PATIENCE

"Love is patient" (v. 4). Don't get in a hurry. Your marriage did not fall apart overnight, and it will not be rebuilt today. Don't set time limits for yourself or your spouse. "If you don't come back by the first of the month, you can forget it!" is not a loving expression. When you set limits, you are trying to dominate the other person. You are telling him what he must do. That may be part of the reason you are presently separated. None of us likes to be dominated. We operate best when we are free. You don't really want your spouse to come back because of a threat. You want him or her to come of his own volition. Give him time. Express your desire, but step back and let him decide.

Be patient also with your spouse's ambivalence. During separation, individuals are emotionally pulled in two directions. Some desire, however faint, for the fulfillment of earlier dreams calls for reconciliation. On the other hand, there is the pain and hurt of a sick marriage that emotionally pushes him or her away. There may also be someone else to whom he is attracted, thus the emotional pull in that direction. A person may sincerely say one thing today and something else tomorrow. He is not intending to lie. He is simply reporting his feelings at the moment. It is to be hoped that he or she will learn not to make decisions based upon feelings, but upon what is right. In the meantime, however, you must be patient with his contradictory statements. The expression of understanding is even more helpful: "I understand that you are pulled in two directions. I feel that myself sometimes."

KINDNESS

"Love is kind" (v. 4). The word that is here translated "kind" means "to be useful or beneficial." Thus, kindness may be words or actions that are useful or beneficial to the other person. What can you say or do that will be useful or beneficial to your spouse? If you are a husband who has left, there are scores of things around the house you could do for your wife if she is willing. If your wife has left you, you may still be able to do some "useful or beneficial" things to make her life more pleasant. Don't hold back simply because she walked out on you. If she will allow, you can be God's agent of love toward her. What is to be gained by not helping her? If you don't, someone else will, and you will have missed an opportunity to express love by being kind.

"Love edifies" (1 Corinthians 8:1). The word *edify* means to "build up." One way to edify your spouse is to express kindness in your speech. Say something that is useful or beneficial—something that will build up rather than tear down. Much of our normal conversation while separated is destructive. We express our hostile feelings with cutting words that emphasize the failures of our spouses. Reconciliation is paved with words of kindness. You are both having a struggle with self-image. You both feel badly about what happened. You both feel guilty because of your own failures. Why not build up your spouse by complimenting him on some of the good you see in him?

Some time ago, I read the story of a woman who went to a marriage counselor and confided that she wanted to divorce her husband. "I want to hurt him in the worst possible way," she said. "What do you suggest?"

The counselor replied, "Start showering him with compliments. When he thinks you love him devotedly, then start the divorce action. That's the way to hurt him most."

She returned in two months to report that she had followed his advice.

"Good," said the counselor, "now is the time to file for divorce."

"Divorce!" cried the woman. "Never! I've fallen in love with the guy!"

What had happened? She had started expressing love to him by using compliments. In time, he began to feel loved and began to express love to her.

Yes, warm emotions can be reborn. But kind words and acts must precede warm emotions. Many couples feel that a trial separation will help them get their feelings straightened out. They want to separate and have no contact to see if time apart will cause the warm feelings to return. Such a process is futile. Attitude and action must precede positive emotions. Distance alone will not turn emotions around.

What kind thing could you do or say today that would help your spouse? How about a phone call to express interest in how he or she is doing? Don't make this a daily thing, unless the partner desires, but once in a while it can be an expression of love. Your mate may even say, "Please don't call," when all the while he or she hopes you will. You do not want to badger each

63

other, but a friendly call to share concern for your spouse's well-being is a gesture of love. Remember, you are working for reconciliation. Love is a powerful step in the right direction.

Don't Envy Your Spouse

"Love does not envy" (v. 4). Each spouse usually thinks the other has the best end of the bargain while separated. The wife with children will complain that her husband is free to do what he pleases whereas she must stay at home with the children. The husband complains that with all the money she demands, he can't afford to live, let alone enjoy life.

The envy game leads a wife to have an affair because her husband does. It leads the husband to skip town, forsaking his responsibility for children, to get away and find happiness. The truth is that separation is rough on both of you. Neither of you has an ideal situation. There are added pressures on both. Finances, logistics, loneliness, meaning to life, all cry for answers. You are living in an abnormal state. Husband and wife were not made to live separated. They were made to live in family unity. Emotionally, physically, spiritually, and socially your best interests are served in seeking to reconcile your differences and finding marital unity. Don't envy your mate's position, but pray and work toward the union of two halves now separated and hurting.

Don't Proclaim Your Own Righteousness

"Love does not boast, it is not proud" (v. 4). It is so easy to look back and announce all of your righteous acts in the marriage while overlooking your weaknesses. "I was faithful to you. I cooked your meals, washed your shirts, cared for your children, and where did it get me? You cannot say that I did not try. I begged you to spend more time with me. I was willing to go with you anywhere, any time. I— I— I—." Such talk may be true, but it is not loving.

Your past record speaks for itself. You do not need to toot your own horn. Your friends know you. Your children know you. You know the truth about yourself. God knows you totally. And your spouse knows you, though he/she may choose to accentuate the negative at the present time. Love will refuse to proclaim its own goodness.

BE COURTEOUS

"Love is not rude" (v. 5). The opposite of rudeness is courtesy. You do not have to treat each other rudely simply because you are separated. The word *courtesy* means "courtlike in manners." Treat your spouse with dignity and respect as if you were courting. He is estranged, and you are seeking to win his affection. Can you remember how you treated him before marriage? If it was respectful, then return to those actions and words.

There is no reason for arguing and screaming when you are together. "A gentle answer turns away wrath, but a harsh word stirs up anger" (Proverbs 15:1). Certainly you need to discuss issues, but you do not need to attack each other in the process. I know you sometimes get angry, but we are instructed not to sin in our anger (Ephesians 4:26). For practical suggestions on how to communicate constructively in the midst of conflict see the section on communication in my book *Toward A Growing Marriage* (see Appendix).

If your mate is open to the idea, why not arrange for a series of "dates"? Don't feel that you must always discuss your problems. Do things that you enjoy doing together. While together, treat each other with courtesy. Do those little things that you know the other appreciates. Speak with kindness. Put the other's interests first. Rediscover each other's assets.

AVOID SELFISHNESS

"Love is not self-seeking" (v. 5). Love does not demand its own way. When most of us got married, we were thinking of what we would get out of the marriage. We had dreams of our own happiness and of what our mates would do for us. Certainly we wanted them to be happy also, but our chief thoughts were on what marriage would mean to us.

After the wedding we found that our mates did not always

think of our happiness. They did not always meet our needs. More and more they demanded our time, energy, and resources for their own happiness. We felt cheated and used. So we fought for our rights. We demanded that our spouses do certain things for us, or we gave up and sought happiness elsewhere.

Happiness is a unique commodity. *It is never found by the person shopping for it.* You may search the shelves of the whole world for personal happiness and never find it at any price. Lonely men and women in every age have grumbled and complained at the futility of their search for happiness. *Genuine happiness is the by-product of making someone else happy.* Do not the Scriptures say, "It is more blessed to give than to receive" (Acts 20:35)?

What can you do for the happiness of your spouse? "I don't want him/her to be happy," you admit. *"I want to be happy!"* A worthy objective indeed, but how will you find happiness? You must discover the needs of someone else and seek to meet those needs. Why not begin with your spouse? Why not ask him/her to talk to you about his/her greatest needs in life? Listen carefully and ask: "How could I meet some of those needs?" Your spouse may not allow you to fulfill that objective, but you will be better for having tried. You will find yourself further down the road of happiness than when you resented your spouse and refused to reach out to offer help.

FORGET THE PAST

"Love keeps no record of wrongs" (v. 5). How many times in a counseling session have I listened as a husband or wife spent hours detailing the past words and actions of his or her spouse? Some can go back and replay the minute details of events that happened fifteen years ago. Each time they replay the event they relive the emotions of the moment. The hurt, pain, and disappointment are all felt as though it happened yesterday. I ask you, of what value is that? It is fine to share it once with a counselor, but to replay it daily in your own mind is worse than useless. It is destructive.

66

All of us have failures in our closets that could be pulled out by our mates and used to destroy us. Yes, we are guilty of horrible failures, but the great message of the Bible is that there is forgiveness. Christ died for our sins, so that we might be free from condemnation. "There is therefore now no condemnation for those who are in Christ Jesus" (Romans 8:1). Forgiveness means that God no longer holds our sins against us. He never reminds us of past failures.

We need to follow God's example in the treatment of our spouses. Yes, we have been wronged, but we have the power to forgive. If your mate confesses and asks forgiveness, you must never again bring up the past. No positive purpose is served by bringing up specifics again and again. Your well-being is not determined by the past, but by what you do with the future. What is important is how you treat each other today, not how you treated each other last month.

TRUST

"Love always trusts" (v. 6). "Can I ever trust him again?" a wife asks. "How can I learn to trust her after what has happened?" asks a sincere husband. Trust is an essential ingredient to marital unity. When we trust our mates we believe in their basic integrity. We feel that what they say is true. We have no reason to doubt. When an individual violates our confidence and is not truthful, however, trust is fractured. When that happens more than once, trust diminishes and in time disintegrates.

Can trust be reborn? Yes, if integrity is reborn. Trust dies when integrity dies. If we will confess our sins and ask forgiveness, we are forgiven by God. It is to be hoped that our mates will also forgive us. At that moment the seed of integrity is planted again. It takes time, however, for trust to come to fruition. Trust was not destroyed overnight, and it will not flourish immediately. Yes, we can come to trust again, but such trust will be built upon a record of integrity. It takes time to establish such a record. We must water the tender plant of integrity until its roots sink deeply into our relationships again.

67

"Love always hopes" (v. 6). I think the greatest thing a counselor brings to the counseling room is hope. A listening ear, a caring heart, communication skills, biblical teachings—all are necessary to successful counseling, but without hope all will fail. That spirit of hope was born out of my own marriage and encouraged by the hundreds of couples whom I have seen find wholeness. It is rooted in the powerful teachings of the Bible.

In the early years of our marriage, Karolyn and I despaired of hope. It seemed that our dream would not come true. We loved each other (we thought), but we could not resolve persistent conflicts. We held to our own ideas of what the other should be and do, but neither of us lived up to those expectations. I knew the pain of seeing the one thing I wanted most in life, a happy marriage, seemingly slipping away with each passing day. We did not physically leave each other, but we were separated emotionally.

There was no simple solution, no magic wand that changed our lives, but we stayed with each other until attitudes changed. Books, conferences, friends, and God all worked together to help us see that much of our destructive behavior grew out of our own insecurities. We came to understand ourselves better, the assets and liabilities of our own personalities. We started listening instead of talking. Asking instead of demanding. Seeking to understand rather than seeking to get our own ways. We came to appreciate each other's strengths and to help each other in the weak areas. We came to see ourselves as friends. The warmth and security of our moments together now are a long way from the pain and hurt of those earlier years, but I remember, and I have hope for others.

The gospel of Christ is the power of God unto salvation to all who believe (Romans 1:16). Through the years I have seen lives changed radically whenever men and women have committed themselves to Christ. The simple message of the gospel is that not only will God forgive our sins through our faith in what Christ did on the cross, but that the Spirit of Christ will actually come to live in us and give us power to change. All men and women have the power to change, but the Christian has the specific help of the Holy Spirit when he/she chooses to walk God's way.

Yes, there is hope for you and hope for your marriage. The first step is to turn your life over to God, and the second step is to love your spouse in spite of all that has happened. Certainly there is the real possibility that your mate will not respond to your love or to the love of God. But God will not leave you without hope. " 'For I know the plans that I have for you,' declares the LORD, 'plans for welfare and not for calamity to give you a future and a hope' " (Jeremiah 29:11).

You have a future with God. That future involves every effort toward reconciliation. God will direct your steps in fruitful living. Your ultimate fulfillment is not dependent upon the response of your mate, but upon your own response to God.

GROWTH ASSIGNMENTS

1. Think prayerfully as you make a list of specific ways you could express God's love to your spouse.
2. Make another list of the things you must stop doing or saying if you are to be God's agent of love toward your spouse.
3. Pray that God will enable you to cease all destructive words and actions toward your spouse.
4. Select one of the actions you listed under number 1 above and ask God for an opportunity to express His love to your spouse this week.
5. Commit yourself to walk with God regardless of what your spouse does.

7

How Will I Handle the Loneliness?

Some weeks ago, I spoke to our congregation on the role of single adults in the family of God. In describing some of the problems faced by singles, I mentioned the pain of loneliness. The following week, I was approached by a young mother, separated from her husband, who said, "I don't think you know what you're talking about." I was taken aback for a moment. "What do you mean?" I asked.

"Your sermon last week about loneliness—I don't think you have any idea what it means to be lonely. You have a wife who loves you. How could you know what it is like to be lonely?"

I acknowledged that she was quite right. "I'm certain that I do not know the pain you are going through," I admitted. There is a sense in which no one knows the pain that another experiences. We can only listen to those who hurt and try to understand.

I reflected on the words I had written some months before when I was away from my family for three weeks while teaching a course on single adult ministries at a West Coast college: "It has been a long time since I have felt the loneliness I have experienced this afternoon and evening. Three thousand miles

71

from home and friends gives one a feeling of emptiness. Hundreds of people are on campus, but I know none of them. The students seem to know one another and feel at home. I feel very alone."

The pain I felt that night, the isolation of being unknown by any of the people around me, was nothing compared with the aloneness that young mother felt. I knew that in time I would be coming home to a loving wife and caring children. I envisioned that reunion. I lived with that dream. But that young lady had no such vision, no such dream.

A young man said to his pastor: "I've had two lonely years. I don't mean lonesome; I mean lonely. Do you know the difference between lonesome and lonely? No! You have never had to, because lonesome is when somebody is not there and you know they will be back after a while. Being lonely is when you don't have anybody to be lonesome for. I was lonesome for a long time after they left. But that was when I thought they were coming back. I'm not blaming them. I'm not saying it wasn't my fault. Most of it was. But they are not ever coming back. Not in a million years. You don't know what hell is! And I hope you never do!"

Loneliness is for real! What many do not realize is that it can be deadly. James J. Lynch, professor of psychology and scientific director of the psychosomatic clinic at the University of Maryland School of Medicine, has made an extensive study of the relationship between loneliness and physical health. In an interview, Dr. Lynch was asked how close the connection is between loneliness and health. He responded: "That's like asking what is the connection between air and one's health. Like the air we breathe, human companionship is taken for granted until we are deprived of it. The fact is that social isolation, sudden loss of love and chronic loneliness are significant contributors to illness and premature death. Loneliness is not only pushing our culture to the breaking point, it is pushing our physical health to the breaking point."[1]

Of course, loneliness is not limited to the separated. Many married couples are living in the same house but are isolated

72

emotionally. A recent study was made in Israel by Jack H. Medalie and Uri Goldbourt, which involved 10,000 married men who were forty years of age or older. The study was designed to determine factors contributing to angina pectoris, a type of heart disease. Those men were studied over a five-year period. The study revealed that fewer of those who had loving and supportive wives developed angina pectoris than did those whose wives were "colder" (52 per 1000 versus 93 per 1000).[2] An intimate relationship in marriage enhances physical health. Loneliness within the marital relationship is detrimental to health.

Loneliness for the separated, however, seems to be even more acute. One lady wrote, "Loneliness is perhaps the deepest pit which blocks the path of the separated. After several years of marriage, I missed not having anyone with whom to share the little events of each day. Meal times were especially lonely, and cooking for one seemed pointless. Mothers have children to cook for and talk to, but nonetheless, they long for adult companionship. Not having children myself, I plunged into activities so that I wouldn't have time to reflect on how empty my life was. At church or at a party I often felt isolated, especially if no one made an effort to sit with me."[3]

Robert S. Weiss, professor of sociology at the University of Massachusetts, who has pioneered in the exploration of loneliness, identifies two forms of loneliness—emotional and social.[4] Although the symptoms differ, the cause of both types of loneliness remains the same: the inability to satisfy the need to form meaningful attachments.

Emotional loneliness springs from the need for intimacy with a spouse or a best friend. A person who is emotionally lonely feels that there is no one he can absolutely count on. Symptoms include feelings of tension, vigilance against possible threat, restlessness, loss of appetite, an inability to fall asleep, and a pervasive low-level anxiety.

In social loneliness the individual experiences a sense of detachment from the community at large. He experiences the feeling that "what matters is taking place elsewhere."[5] Often the divisions of the day become meaningless to the socially lonely. They may doze in the middle of the day and awake in the middle of the night. Social loneliness is especially pronounced among individuals who have no significant vocation. They sense that their lives are not accomplishing anything worthwhile.

The separated are likely to experience both kinds of loneliness. That is especially true when one does not have a social support system outside the marriage. The wife who has been at home through the years will likely feel cut off not only from her husband but from the whole world when separation occurs.

Loneliness is sometimes mistaken for depression. Though lonely people may eventually become depressed out of frustration at their inability to dispel loneliness, the two are very different states: depression resists change; loneliness produces pressure to change. Depression renders one immobile, whereas loneliness will press one to move in any direction that offers hope. That is why many lonely people move toward singles bars, feeling all the while that they should not go. Depression keeps one at home with all the shades drawn in self-pity.

Social Loneliness

Social loneliness, that feeling of being cut off from all that is significant in the world, may be cured when you become involved in a meaningful vocation. Much of our sense of worth comes from what we are doing with our lives. If I feel that my life is making a genuine positive contribution to God and the world, I am not likely to be troubled with social loneliness. I am not cut off, but have become an active meaningful part of what is significant in my generation.

For some, that may mean going back to school to prepare for the vocational dream that has been dormant many years. I am reminded of one wife in her middle thirties who upon separation enrolled in the local technical institute, finished her high school work, developed secretarial skills, and now feels very much a part of her vocational community. The sense of belong-

74

ing to a team that is making a significant contribution to the world brings emotional healing from social loneliness.

Such training may also build your self-confidence. As you demonstrate that you can be successful in the classroom you feel better about yourself, and you stretch your vision of what God may have for you in the future. You doubtless have many undeveloped interests and abilities. This may be the best possible time to begin their cultivation.

Such vocational and personal development may well serve as a stepping stone to reconciliation to your spouse. As he or she sees you seizing the opportunity for growth rather than succumbing to the paralysis of suffering, he is more likely to see hope for a more mature marriage. Your mate can see you becoming a different and better person. Such constructive change brings a breath of fresh hope. On the other hand, your positive action does not guarantee his or her return. What it does guarantee is the healing of social loneliness.

Some separated mothers will feel such vocational training is impossible or undesirable. They feel limited or fenced in by the children. Let me remind you that children are a blessing of God (Psalm 127:3). They are no less a blessing when you experience separation. You will be spared much of the loneliness that others experience because of your relationship with your children. In terms of significant vocation, none is more rewarding than training children. Many other vocations involve working with "things," but you are dealing with *persons*. Your commodity is eternal; theirs is temporal. It is still true that "the hand that rocks the cradle rules the world." In my opinion, it is tragic that so many mothers have relinquished the greatest vocation for lesser pursuits. Do not decry your situation if you cannot work outside the home. Thank God for your opportunity and make the most of the greatest.

On the other hand, some mothers who do not desire to work outside the home are forced to do so by the separation. The husband cannot or will not provide adequate financial support, and the wife is pressured to work. If you feel such pressure, view it as an opportunity rather than an oppression. Ask God to give added physical and emotional strength. Ask for the wisdom of Solomon in training your children and move out to be God's woman. Social loneliness will not be one of your problems.

For those who cannot work or go to school, there are many opportunities for involvement in meaningful projects in your community. Civic groups are always looking for volunteers who are willing to invest time and energy. Christian groups such as Christian women's clubs and Christian businessmen's committees will help channel your abilities into meaningful activities. You need not stay on the sidelines—you can be on the team! You can have the sense of accomplishment that comes from a wise investment of your life.

EMOTIONAL LONELINESS

The ultimate answer to emotional loneliness, the lack of an intimate relationship with another person, is to reach out and establish wholesome contact with yourself, God, and others. We have discussed all of those in previous chapters, but let me say again that you have the capacity to be your own best friend. You spend more time with yourself than anyone else. Why not make the time pleasant? Learn to like yourself and create an atmosphere in which you can enjoy life. You need not destroy yourself because of what has happened. You have admitted your failures—now get up and do something today that will make you feel pleased with yourself.

The church can greatly assist you in making meaningful contact with God and others. It is a joy to observe what happens when a lonely separated person enters the life of our church. In the sermon he hears hope, which he has not heard for many weeks. In the informal study groups he meets people who are finding that hope for themselves. He discovers people who are not perfect, but forgiven, who reach out to him in love. Week by week, little by little, a person comes to respond to God and to those hands of hope. He learns to talk to God and to hear His word for him. He learns to share himself with others

76

who genuinely care. In time the loneliness fades, and the beauty of that once dejected individual begins to unfold like a fragrant rose. Few things are more rewarding for those of us who minister in the fellowship of a local church.

Does it sound too easy? Too religious? I assure you, it is neither easy nor otherworldly. In the first place there is a great deal of risk on your part. You must move out from the bondage of your cocoon. Yes, you can learn to fly, but the cocoon must go. You can learn freedom from loneliness, but you must leave your room in search of a caring fellowship. Unfortunately, you will not find the warmth you need in all churches. Some groups have become a mutual aid society for those who pay their dues, rather than a lighthouse for battered ships. But don't give up. Jesus said, "Ask, and it shall be given to you; seek, and you shall find; knock, and it shall be opened to you" (Matthew 7:7-8). Your searching will not be in vain.

One warning as you go. Seek Christian love, not marriage. Remember, your goal is reconciliation with your spouse. You want to keep all roads open in that direction. In the meantime, you need the love and care of others. Again, don't expect perfection in those whom you meet at church. You may even find individuals in the church who will try to exploit you. The church does not stand at the door to check the character of all who attend its activities. As Jesus said, the wheat and the weeds grow together until the time of harvest (Matthew 13:24-30).

Of all the social institutions of our nation, no organization is better equipped to care for the needs of the lonely than the church. The church offers not only a social support system, but a spiritual support system as well. To be rightly related to God and warmly related to His creatures is the best medication available for loneliness.

Let me digress a moment and say a word to church members. We must accept the challenge of creating the kind of fellowship I have described above. It is desperately tragic when hurting people come to our services and leave without a healing touch. As one older woman put it, "I sit in the pew next to a warm body, but I draw no heat. I am in the same faith, but draw no act of love. I sing the same hymns with those next to me, but I hear only my own voice. When it is finished, I leave, as I came in, hungry for a touch of someone, someone to tell me I am a person worth something to them. Just a smile would do it perhaps, some gesture or sign that I am not a stranger."[6]

As Paul Tournier said,

> It is the church alone, nevertheless, which can answer the world of today's tremendous thirst for community. Christ sent His disciples two by two. The great body of the early Christians, according to the Bible, "were of one heart and soul; they had all things in common" (Acts 4:32; 2:44). Instead of demonstrating the way to fellowship to the world today, the church seems to embody the triumph of individualism. The faithful sit side by side without even knowing each other; the elders gather in a little parliament with its parties and formalities; the pastors do their work without reference to one another.[7]

May we never be satisfied until the churches with whom we minister see themselves carrying on the ministry of our Lord who said, "Come to Me, all who are weary and heavy-laden, and I will give you rest" (Matthew 11:28).

Whether you meet people at church, in your community, or at the grocery store, you must take the initiative in reaching out to others. Emotional loneliness will not go away simply with the passing of time. You need the fellowship of others, and you must take the initiative in establishing relationships.

Others may not come to you, but as you express interest in others by initiating conversation, they will become interested in you. When you show concern for the well being of others, you will find that concern being returned to you. As you build caring relationships, emotional loneliness dissipates.

As the title of James Johnson's thoughtful book so pungently proclaims, loneliness is not forever. You may feel locked into a hopeless situation. You are separated, but not divorced. Free to hurt, but not to remarry. Lonely and alone. But just as separation is a temporary state, so loneliness is only a passageway—a hallway, not a living room. On one end of the hall is

78

depression, immobility, pain, and darkness, but on the other is life, love, and meaning. You are in the middle of the hallway. Perhaps you are even lying on the floor crying. But eventually, you will get up. When you do, I hope you will start walking (perhaps crawling at first) toward the door of hope. Just through that door are some loving people who will accept you as you are and help you become what you want to be. Loneliness is not forever!

GROWTH ASSIGNMENTS

1. Clarify your feelings of social loneliness by answering the following:
   a) Do you feel cut off, removed from all that is worthwhile in the world?
   b) Do you see others accomplishing meaningful goals while you sit in the stands and watch?
   c) If you could do anything in the world with your life, what would you like to do?
   d) Is that goal realistic for you? If not, what would be a realistic goal?
   e) If you were to accomplish that goal, what would be the first step?
   f) How will that step affect your relationship with your spouse?
   g) What will such a step do for you?
   h) Why not take that step and ask God to steer you into what is best?

2. Clarify your feelings of emotional loneliness by answering the following:
   a) Do you feel emotionally alone? That there is no one with whom you can share your honest feelings?
   b) What opportunity and freedom do you have to share your feelings with your spouse?
   c) Is there a friend with whom you can share without fear of being rejected? If so, have you shared your present pain with that friend? Why not do so today?

d) Do you feel the need to develop friendships with others? Where, in your community, could you go to develop such friendships?

e) Are you presently involved in a Christian fellowship? If not, what keeps you from doing so immediately?

3. If loneliness is acute, and you have been unable to share with anyone, you may want to make an appointment with a counselor or pastor, who can help you see your situation more objectively.

Notes

1. James J. Lynch in an interview with Christopher Anderson, *People*, 22 August 1977, p. 30.
2. Maya Pines, "Psychological Hardness: The Role of Challenge in Health," *Psychology Today*, December 1980, p. 43.
3. "Divorce", *Christian Medical Society Journal*, 7, no. 1 (Winter 1976): 30.
4. Robert S. Weiss, *The Experience of Emotional and Social Isolation* (Cambridge: Massachusetts Institute of Technology, 1973), p. 54.
5. Ibid., p. 57.
6. James Johnson, *Loneliness Is Not Forever* (Chicago: Moody, 1979), p. 21.
7. Paul Tournier, *Escape From Loneliness* (Philadelphia: Westminster, 1976), p. 23.

8

What About My Bitterness?

"I am so angry when I think of him. When I think of all that he has done to me, I literally hate him. I get furious when I think about it. I know it's not right, but I can't help it."

"When I saw the guy she was dating, I'll have to be honest, my first thought was to kill both of them."

Such thoughts and feelings are not uncommon. Psychologists indicate that an individual in the process of separation and divorce goes through the same emotional stages he would experience if a death had occurred. One of those stages is anger. That anger may be directed at self, God, or the spouse, and is to some degree directed at all three. Human emotions have often been divided into three basic areas: love, fear, and hostility. Love is a feeling that moves us *toward* a person, place, or thing. Fear moves us *away from* something or someone. Hostility is a feeling *against* the person, place, or thing.

When we come to the point of separation, usually one or both spouses have lost their love feelings. Fear may or may not be a prominent feeling, but hostility is almost always present. We have been hurt. We have been wronged. Our spouses are responsible, and our hostile feelings are directed toward them.

We want to strike back at them and make them suffer as we have.

Usually both individuals feel some anger, since each views the other as responsible for his pain. Though anger is normal, it is also destructive. Anger may destroy its object, but more often it destroys the one who harbors it. If anger can be expressed in a wholesome constructive manner, it can lead to desired change, but if left to smolder within, it can be devastating. Unexpressed anger produces death, like a malignant cancer slowly destroying life's fiber.

Uncontrolled expression of anger is like an explosion that destroys everything in its range. To rant and rave, scream and shout, jump and kick serves no constructive purpose. Such an outburst is like an emotional heart attack and may produce permanent damage.

If explosive anger is like a heart attack and repressed anger like cancer, then obviously our best alternative is confessed anger. The word *confess* means "to agree with." When we confess anger, we agree that we are angry. We are not trying to hide our feelings, nor are we giving full vent to our heat, but we are seeking a constructive way to release the pressure.

The Scriptures are extremely clear at this point. Paul urges, "Be angry, and yet do not sin; do not let the sun go down on your anger, and do not give the devil an opportunity" (Ephesians 4:26-27). Note Paul does not say, "Don't get angry!" That would be unrealistic. All of us experience feelings of anger when we think we have been mistreated. Rather, Paul says, "In your anger, do not sin!" Don't be so controlled by your feelings of anger that you do or say something destructive and thus sinful. The implication is that we are to be responsible for our actions even when we are angry. Thus the challenge: When you are angry, don't sin!

Anger makes one very prone to sinful behavior. If we simply do what comes naturally we will lash out against the person or object of our anger. Most murders occur in an atmosphere of anger or drunkenness, and sometimes both. Most murderers did not intend to kill. They simply lost control of their emotions.

82

I have heard husbands who physically abused their wives, weeping and repeating, "I didn't mean to do it. I didn't mean to do it." Wives and husbands who verbally abuse each other often say afterward, "I regret the things I said. I wish I could recall my words. I did not mean what I said."

The challenge is to refuse to be controlled by your feelings of anger. Confess your anger to yourself, God, a friend, or a counselor and to your spouse, but don't be controlled by it. When you talk about your feelings with someone else, you dissipate the anger and are far more likely to do something constructive. The second part of Paul's challenge is: Don't let the sun go down while you are still angry. Anger is not to be tolerated as a permanent guest. It may appear on center stage for a brief moment, but it must not be allowed to interrupt the drama of your life.

The best way to get rid of anger is to confess it. The worst thing you can do is to repress it. When you hold it in and tell yourself that you are not angry, you are setting the stage for a volcanic eruption of gigantic proportions. In short, you are setting yourself up for sin. You are giving the devil a foothold.

Bitterness is nothing more than repressed anger. It is anger held in so long that it becomes a fixed way of thinking and feeling. You become locked into constant thoughts of how you might hurt your spouse. You play the record of past failures over and over again. Each time you feel the hurt, the pain, the anger as though it just happened. Again and again you ask the same questions and get the same answers. The recording plays until the grooves are etched deeply into your mind. Anger has developed into bitterness, and you are now filled with the malignancy of hate. You say that your spouse has made your life miserable, but in reality you have chosen the company of anger. No one can embrace anger without becoming infected with bitterness and hatred.

The Freedom of Forgiveness

If your anger has developed into bitterness, you will likely need the assistance of a counselor or pastor to help you extract the infection and lead you to the healing waters of God's forgiveness. Yes, you have a right to feel angry, but you do not have the right to destroy one of God's creatures—yourself. In the Bible bitterness is always viewed as sin. The feeling of anger cannot be avoided, but bitterness results from daily choosing to let anger live in your heart. Thus we read, "Get rid of all bitterness, rage and anger, brawling and slander, along with every form of malice" (Ephesians 4:31, NIV). We must confess bitterness as sin and accept God's forgiveness.

We should note that a one-time confession of bitterness may not alleviate all hostile feelings. If the bitterness has been there a long time, the feelings that accompany the bitter attitude may die slowly. What do you do when thoughts and feelings of anger and bitterness return? Acknowledge those thoughts and feelings to God and affirm your commitment to forgive. An appropriate prayer might be: "Father, You know my thoughts and feelings, but I thank You that with Your help, I will no longer hold those things against my spouse. Now help me as I move out to be an agent of Your love." Forgiveness will need to be a daily discipline, and you must refuse to harbor resentment. As you practice forgiveness, the angry, bitter thoughts and feelings will occur less and less.

Once freed from bitterness, we are challenged to "be kind to one another, tender-hearted, forgiving each other, just as God in Christ also has forgiven you. . . . Be imitators of God" (Ephesians 4:32–5:1). We must not stop with acknowledging our bitterness and accepting God's forgiveness. We must also forgive our spouses for those things that originally brought anger to the surface. God is not only concerned that we be freed from anger, but that we be agents of love and kindness as we discussed earlier.

That is the marvelous message of the Bible. God does not want us to be enslaved to any negative emotion. Rather, He wants us to have a love relationship with Him that will spill over into our relationships with others. Anger focuses on an area of conflict in our relationship. We are to seek to resolve that conflict. If our spouses will not help us deal with that conflict, we must refuse to be victims of anger. We may allow anger entrance into our lives, but we cannot allow it to take up residence.

THE DANGER OF RETALIATION

Uncontrolled bitterness has a way of fostering revenge. When we yield to the "get even" spirit, we are violating the clear teaching of Scripture. Paul says, "Never pay back evil for evil to anyone. Respect what is right in the sight of all men. . . . Never take your own revenge, beloved, but leave room for the wrath of God, for it is written, 'VENGEANCE IS MINE, I WILL REPAY,' says the Lord" (Romans 12:17, 19). You may have been greatly wronged by your spouse, but it is not your responsibility to punish him for his sin. He must face God with his sin, and God is a just judge.

Again Paul says to the Thessalonian Christians, "See that no one repays another with evil for evil, but always seek after that which is good for one another and for all men" (1 Thessalonians 5:15). The emphasis is upon seeking what is good for your spouse, not upon getting even. Seeking his good is not the same as overlooking his sin. It is not good to allow your spouse to continue an irresponsible, sinful life-style. You are to seek his or her good, not with angry threats, but with kind admonitions.

Anger and bitterness are often expressed in destructive verbal explosions. "Speak when you are angry," said Ambrose Bierce, "and you will make the best speech you will ever regret." Verbal retaliation accomplishes no constructive purpose. Far better to confess that we are angry and therefore cannot discuss the issue positively and prefer to wait until we can handle our feelings. Issues need to be discussed; conflicts need to be resolved; but we will find no solution in the heat of anger.

Don't condemn yourself for feeling angry. That feeling indicates that you are a member of the human race. You have the capacity to become deeply moved about something you think important. Great! Let that concern lead you to constructive action. Don't become enslaved to your anger and do something

85

that will make the situation worse. Acknowledge your feelings of anger to God and a friend and ask both to help you respond creatively and redemptively to the situation.

Growth Assignments

1. Express your anger in writing. Ask God to guide you as you try to express your feelings. You may begin, "I am angry because . . ."
2. Think of a friend who will be objective, with whom you may share what you have written. Ask him or her to listen as you read and then to help you find constructive ways to deal with the issue.
3. Do you feel that you have allowed your anger to develop into bitterness? If so, are you willing to confess it as sin and accept God's forgiveness?
4. If you have never invited Christ into your life, as you confess your sin, why not invite Him to come into your life and give you power to deal with your present problems?

9

If Your Spouse Returns

Sometimes an individual says to his partner, "I want you to be happy. If leaving will make you happy, then leave. It hurts, but I want you to be happy." On the surface that may sound very loving and self-sacrificing, but in reality it is neither. Love seeks the good of the spouse. According to the Scriptures it is not good for them to break their marital vows and to leave. Therefore, they should not be encouraged to do so.

THE CHOICE TO RETURN

Righteousness, not happiness, leads to man's greatest good. If happiness is found by doing what is wrong, that happiness will be momentary indeed. The pleasures of sin are always short-lived. Thus, the Christian must never encourage his/her spouse to leave in pursuit of happiness. Instead, he must encourage righteousness. What does the Bible teach us to do in our present situation? What is right from God's perspective? If you cannot readily answer those questions, then you should seek the help of a godly pastor who is acquainted with biblical principles for personal relationships. Once we know what is right, then we must seek it at all costs.

Doing what is right may not be the easiest route, but it will always be the best route. It may seem easier to separate and pursue your own happiness than to work at reconciling differences and rediscovering love. It may be much harder to stay together than to separate, especially when feelings of love have gone. The Christian's call is not to the easy road, but to the right road. I can promise you that the right road leads to both happiness and love after the pain of reconciliation.

The choice to return to your spouse and pursue reconciliation is a step of faith. But it is not blind faith. It is faith based upon the counsel of God. You cannot see the warmth of emotional love returning. You cannot see differences resolved. You cannot see the intimacy that you desire from a marriage. You must take the first steps, therefore, by faith, not by sight. With your hand in God's hand, you must walk with Him, trusting His wisdom. What you see will be only through the eyes of faith. In so doing, you walk the road with the great men and women of the past.

Take Moses, for example. "By faith Moses, when he had grown up, refused to be called the son of Pharaoh's daughter; choosing rather to endure ill-treatment with the people of God, than to enjoy the passing pleasures of sin; considering the reproach of Christ greater riches than the treasures of Egypt; for he was looking to the reward" (Hebrews 11:24-26). Moses grew up in Pharaoh's household. He was in line for the wealth and prestige of Egypt, but God's plan called for him to deliver his fellow Israelites. By faith, Moses chose to walk with God. The only assurance he had that things would turn out for the best was the promise of God. That is the assurance you have. Do you need more?

Reconciliation demands a choice. It is a choice against continued separation and ultimate divorce. It is a choice to reaffirm your marital vows and actively seek to discover the intimacy and fulfillment God had in mind when He instituted marriage. It is not a choice to go back to the kind of relationship you had when you separated, but to work toward establishing something far more meaningful.

The choice for reconciliation is not popular in our day. A thousand voices will seek to allure you to the supposed happiness of divorce and remarriage. Others will call you to join them in sex without commitment. You stand at the crossroads. The decision is yours. Robert Frost described the significance of decisions when he wrote:

Two roads diverged in a yellow wood
And sorry I could not travel both
And be one traveler, long I stood
And looked down one as far as I could,
To where it bent in the undergrowth;

Then took the other, as just as fair,
And having perhaps the better claim,
Because it was grassy and wanted wear,
Though as for that, the passing there,
Had worn them really about the same,

And both that morning equally lay
In leaves no step had trodden black.
Oh, I kept the first for another day!
Yet knowing how way leads on to way,
I doubted if I should ever come back.

I shall be telling this with a sigh
Somewhere ages and ages hence:
Two roads diverged in a wood,
And I—
I took the one less traveled by,
And that has made all the difference.

Reconciliation is definitely the road less traveled by, but it too will make all the difference.

STEPS IN RECONCILIATION

Let us assume that you have made your choice in favor of reconciliation. Let me walk with you down that road "less traveled by." First, before you take another step, why not tell God about your decision? Yes, He knows your heart and thus your decision, but God is a person, and He likes to hear your voice. It may seem awkward to pray aloud if you are not accustomed to such conversation, but go ahead. Tell Him how you feel, where you have been, what you have done. Confess your failures and ask for forgiveness. Tell Him of your decision to seek reconciliation with your spouse, and ask for His help. (Remem-

89

ber, He will not force your spouse to reciprocate, but He will enable you to be loving in your attempts.) Ask Him to change you into the person He wants you to be. Ask for guidance as you walk the road to reconciliation.

With the assurance of God's forgiveness and God's help you will now want to share your decision with your spouse. If possible, that should be done in person and not on the phone. Perhaps you could call and invite your spouse for dinner. If he or she is reluctant, tell him that you have something very important you would like to discuss with him. If he insists that you tell him on the phone, then indicate to him that it is too significant to talk about on the phone. If he cannot have dinner with you now, then perhaps you can get together in a week or so. Do not pressure your spouse to join you for dinner. Express understanding at his or her reluctance, but assure him that you want to see him at his convenience. If you cannot agree on getting together, tell him that you will call again in a week or so. Spend the week praying that God will stimulate his or her will. Again, God will not force the decision, but He will prod, encourage, and motivate.

Most spouses will find the dinner easy to arrange. If your spouse will not agree to see you, continue praying and calling every two or three weeks. Do not tell him about your decision on the phone. Your persistence and patience will eventually indicate your seriousness. When you eventually express your decision to seek reconciliation, he or she will likely take it more seriously. It may be that God will use the intervening time to prepare him for what you have to say.

During or after the dinner, tell your spouse that you have been doing a lot of thinking and praying about your marriage. Indicate that you are coming to understand yourself more fully and that much of your behavior has been controlled by your emotions and attitudes. Tell him you have come to realize that you do not have to be a slave to your feelings and that attitudes can be changed. Admit that you have failed in many ways, and ask forgiveness for those failures.

Tell your spouse that you have been reading a book that has

90

stimulated your thinking and has helped you come to the decision that you want to work on restoring your marriage. You may say, "I know that I will not be able to do this without your help. I understand if you feel reluctant. I know that there is not much in the past that would encourage you to try again. But I do not want us to try as we have tried in the past. I want us to work at something far more meaningful than we have ever had. I want us to take whatever steps are necessary to gain self-understanding and understanding of each other. I know that it will take work, and may be painful, but I am willing to do whatever is necessary."

Indicate that you do not expect an answer right away. You want him or her to think and pray about it. You may want to give him a copy of *Hope for the Separated* and suggest that he read it. Tell him that in reading the book, he will perhaps understand some of the things you have been thinking and your decision to seek reconciliation. Suggest that after your spouse has had sufficient time to think, read, and pray that he or she call you and arrange to get together with you again to discuss things further.

Don't expect all problems to melt after such an evening. You have only taken the first step on the road less traveled by. Where do you go from here?

IF WE BOTH ARE WILLING

In chapter 10 we will discuss what you must do if your spouse is not willing to work toward reconciliation. In this chapter, let us assume that your spouse responds affirmatively. He or she is as willing as you are to work at restoring the dream you had when you were married. Should you move back into the same apartment or house immediately? Probably not. Remember, your objective is not to "get back together." Your objective is to give rebirth to your marriage. The conflicts, frustrations, misunderstandings, and unmet needs that led you to separate must be examined and resolved.

For most couples, the process of restoration will require the services of a pastor or marriage counselor. You need to develop skills in expressing your feelings in a constructive way. You must come to understand and appreciate the thoughts and feelings of your spouse. You must find ways to meet each other's emotional and physical needs. Marriage counselors and many pastors are trained in helping you develop such skills.

If you are attending a church, why not call your pastor and tell him of your decision to seek reconciliation and ask if he would have time to help you learn how to relate to each other creatively, or if he could recommend someone who could. Not all pastors are skilled in marriage counseling, but most will be able to direct you to help if they cannot help you. As you meet with the pastor or counselor and develop your communication skills you will begin to feel freedom in your relationship. You will begin to feel more understanding. You will begin to reach agreement on issues that have been unresolved conflicts. You will give each other the freedom to disagree on certain issues and yet be kind and loving to each other.

As you begin to see such growth taking place, you will want to discuss and decide when you should move back into the same apartment or house. There is no precise rule, but most couples will be ready to move back together after two or three sessions with the counselor or pastor. Don't stop seeing the counselor when you move back together. That is an important time. It will bring some added pressures, and you will need to concentrate on open, loving communication during those days. Continue with your counseling until you feel you have adequately dealt with unresolved conflict and developed skills in handling disagreements. The communication skills you learn will be important for the rest of your life. You must not neglect them when the crisis of separation is over.

Some couples will not be able to acquire the services of a trained counselor. Fortunately other sources of help are available. Christian books, tapes, and marriage workshops are within reach of almost any couple today. My book *Toward a Growing Marriage* was written to help couples work through all the basic areas of marital adjustment and to find positive principles for living. At the end of each chapter are practical assignments that stimulate communication and understanding. I suggest that a couple read a chapter each week and complete assignments individually and then discuss assignments with each other. Many separated couples are finding that process extremely beneficial in rebuilding their marriages.

Many churches sponsor workshops and seminars on marriage as a part of their educational programs. Ask your pastor what is available in your church. Also, talk with Christian friends about what is available in their churches. Some church in your community likely has something going on that would be of help to you as you seek to rebuild your marriage.

In reading a book or listening to a taped lecture, the value is not only in the ideas expressed, but in the communication that they stimulate. Couples should take notes as they listen and underline as they read and then tell each other what impressed them. As you talk to each other, seek to understand what your spouse is saying and feeling. Ask questions to clarify, such as: "Are you saying . . . ?" Repeat what you think your mate said and give him or her a chance to clarify. Express love even when you disagree. Remember, your objective in communication is to understand your spouse, to discover needs, and to find out how you can help meet those needs. If husband and wife concentrate on each other's fulfillment, it will not be long until your marriage will surpass your fondest dreams.

The growth patterns you established through counseling or reading, listening, and attending workshops must become a permanent part of your relationship. Marriages are not static. They are either growing or diminishing. You must continue to do the kind of things that stimulate growth. The title of my book *Toward a Growing Marriage* was chosen deliberately. The ultimate goal is not a "perfect" marriage, but a "growing" marriage. Perfect is hard to define, and even if we reached it, perfection would be momentary. Growth is attainable today and every day. If you are growing there is hope, excitement, and satisfaction. Such growth should continue as long as you live. Thus, your marriage will always be alive.

Let your marriage relationship be the most important thing

in your life. Give each other the number 1 place in your thoughts. Keep God at the center of your relationship. Do something each day to express your love for each other. Minimize the weaknesses of your mate and maximize his or her strengths. Brag about his accomplishments, and he will excel. Love and you will be loved. Apply to your marriage the golden rule of all human relationships: "However you want people to treat you, so treat them . . ." (Matthew 7:12).

GROWTH ASSIGNMENTS

1. No one, including God, will force you to return to your marriage. That is a decision that only you can make. But if you decide, you will have all the help of God at your disposal. You have talked with and observed many who have experienced divorce. Would you be willing to find a couple that has a good marriage and ask them how they obtained it? Perhaps you could interview several married couples and ask what problems they have overcome to find fulfillment.

2. If you decide to take the road "less traveled by" you may want to use the checklist below:

Steps we have taken: *Date*

___*a*)   Made my decision to seek reconciliation   _____

___*b*)   Talked with God about my decision and
          asked for His help   _____

___*c*)   Called my spouse and asked for a dinner
          date   _____

___*d*)   Spouse accepted invitation   _____

___*e*)   Related my decision to my spouse   _____

___*f*)   Spouse agreed to seek reconciliation   _____

___*g*)   Arranged for session with pastor or
          counselor   _____

___*h*)   Did assignments made by counselor   _____

94

__i) Additional counseling sessions   _____

__j) Completed additional communication
       assignments   _____

__k) Moved back to same apartment or house   _____

__l) Additional counseling sessions   _____

__m) Completed additional communication
       assignments   _____

Books we have read and discussed:

1. _____   _____
2. _____   _____
3. _____   _____
4. _____   _____
5. _____   _____

Tapes on marriage we have listened to and discussed:

1. _____   _____
2. _____   _____
3. _____   _____
4. _____   _____
5. _____   _____

Marriage workshops, seminars, or classes we have attended:

1. _____   _____
2. _____   _____
3. _____   _____
4. _____   _____

10

If Your Spouse Demands a Divorce

Reconciliation is not always possible. Your best efforts may meet with coldness, hostility, and eventual failure. Even God was not always able to be reconciled to His people. "For all the adulteries of faithless Israel, I had sent her away and given her a writ of divorce" (Jeremiah 3:8). Reconciliation is not always possible because it requires the response of two people, and neither can force the other to return.

Human freedom is real. God would not force Israel to return. He put pressure on her by allowing her enemies to triumph. He removed His hand of blessing, but God did not force Israel to return. God will never remove man's freedom of choice. We must remember that in our prayers. Many separated Christians have prayed and pleaded with God to "bring my spouse back." The spouse has not returned, so the Christian becomes discouraged and concludes that God does not answer prayer. Many become hostile toward God and critical of the church and Christianity, and thus turn from their only source of real help. But God will not force your spouse to return. He, in response to your prayers, will put pressure on him or her to seek reconciliation, but your spouse may still rebel against God's stimulation and your best efforts.

Does the possibility of failure mean that we should not try? The whole teaching of the Bible stands in opposition to an attitude of futility. God never gives up on His people, and history is replete with examples of genuine spiritual restoration. Marital restoration is worth the risk of failure.

Your attitude is important. Don't say, "I might fail," but rather, "I might succeed!" Few goals are more deserving than the restoration of your marriage. If you can discover not what you had before the separation, but what you dreamed of having when you were married, your efforts will be rewarded. I have never met an individual who sincerely, consistently, and lovingly tried the things I suggest and regretted the effort. I have met scores of individuals who have succeeded and today are happily restored to their mates and growing with them.

Throughout this book, I have tried to be realistic by indicating that you cannot control the response of your mate. You are keeper of your own heart and responsible for your own words and actions. I have indicated that the biblical ideal calls you to seek reconciliation. You must face God with your willingness or refusal to pursue that ideal. Your spouse has the same responsibility. Your choice for reconciliation does not guarantee that your mate will reciprocate. He or she is free to choose.

SHOULD I CONTEST DIVORCE?

If your mate demands divorce there is little if anything to be gained by contesting such action. There was a time when most states required evidence of efforts at conciliation before a divorce would be granted. At this writing, only two states still compel the parties to try for a reconciliation when the ground for divorce is "irreconcilable differences."[1] Forced efforts of reconciliation profit very little, because the blending of lives requires choice, not coercion. Divorce laws in most states are very liberal, and efforts at contesting the divorce result in little except expensive legal fees.

Contesting the divorce is simply a legal step in which one party seeks to prove that the other does not have grounds for divorce. That was feasible when state laws allowed for divorce

98

only on the grounds of insanity, adultery, or abandonment. Today, however, with virtually all states having some form of no-fault divorce laws, such action at most only slows the process a bit. You may ask for time, and some states even require a separation of some months before divorce, but to seek to thwart divorce is futile.

It may seem unfair that if your spouse demands a divorce you have little choice except to go along with that choice, but such is the nature of human relationships. We cannot force anyone to be our friend. Friendship is a mutual choice between two people. If one chooses to dissolve the friendship, the other is helpless to keep it alive. Marriage is the most intimate of all friendships, and it too requires reciprocal action.

You cannot force reconciliation, because by its very nature reconciliation requires two people. Divorce, however, which literally means "to disunite," requires only the action of one. If one person desires union and the other disunion, the one who desires disunion holds the upper hand, for union is impossible without his or her acquiescence.

Do I Need A Lawyer?

Divorce not only severs an emotional and physical relationship, but also a legal contract. Each state has its own laws and regulations regarding the dissolution of a marital contract. In most cases a lawyer will be needed to interpret the laws and guide in the process. California has recently initiated a no-attorney, no-court process for childless couples with no real estate, less than $5,000 in personal property, and less than $2,000 in debt. That streamlined divorce procedure costs only forty to fifty dollars in court fees. Other states may follow California's example, but for most couples a lawyer would be a necessity.

Do spouses need separate lawyers? If your spouse is divorcing you, his or her lawyer will be representing your spouse's interests. If you have had problems agreeing on finances, property, and child-related issues, then you will definitely need a lawyer to represent your interests. If you and your spouse can agree on an equitable settlement, then one attorney can represent both

99

of you. Before you agree on one attorney, however, you should make a trip to the public library and read some of the many books and pamphlets on the legal aspects of divorce. You may also want to talk with several friends who have experienced divorce. That will give you a more realistic idea of what is involved in an equitable settlement.

Our emotions often get in the way of achieving a satisfactory settlement. Ann Diamond, a divorce lawyer, has listed the following situations in which emotions affect a fair settlement:

—A rejected spouse, unable to accept the finality of the separation, may agree to almost any demand of the other party in the hope that it will facilitate a reconciliation.

—A woman accustomed to having her husband make all important decisions will continue to look to him for advice, even though he has left her and is no longer interested in protecting her.

—The long-suffering, passive mate often seeks redress in the settlement for all past miseries of the relationship, whether self-inflicted or otherwise.

—When the break-up is sudden, the rejected spouse may be so traumatized that he, or more frequently, she, is unable to make any realistic estimate of future financial need.

—The spouse who wants out may feel so guilty that he or she will try to compensate by being overly generous in property division and agree to pay or receive support payments which are too high or too low. The subsequent resentment which can erupt in the long run will only cause further problems for both.

—Because the rejected partner may be too depressed to face any additional pressure, he or she will consent to any financial settlement just to get matters over with.

—One spouse may use the children as a means to punish and get even with the rejecting partner.[2]

100

You may need not only legal but emotional help in deciding upon the details of the settlement. As a Christian, you do not want to use the settlement as a punitive club on your spouse. On the other hand, you must be realistic about your needs and what is best for children.

What About the Children?

Tell children the truth about your separation and impending divorce. Don't try to protect them by lying. Eventually they will learn the truth, and if you have lied to them their confidence in you will be diminished. Simply, and with as little embellishment as possible, tell your children what has happened to your marriage. Ideally, both parents should talk with the children together and tell them their decision to divorce. Assure them of your love and tell them that they did not cause the divorce. If your spouse is not willing to join you in talking with the children, then you must do so alone and trust that your spouse will talk with them later.

It is extremely important that the child feel your love. The need to love and be loved is one of the strongest of all human emotions. In childhood, the need to be loved is related directly to the child's sense of security. Without love, the child will be emotionally insecure. Don't assume that your child feels loved simply because you tell him, "I love you." The New Testament challenges us to love not in word only, but in deed (1 John 3:18). Find out what makes your child feel loved. For some children it is sitting close to them and talking; to others it is doing special things for them. Others feel loved when you give them unexpected gifts (that can also be used to exploit parents), whereas others respond to being held physically. Of course, you will want to say the words "I love you" frequently as well.

Both parents should express love to the child in a way that the child understands. If one parent does not express love, however, there is little to be gained by the other parent's verbally assuring the child that the nonloving parent does love him. Actions speak louder than words to children. It is a cheap love whose only evidence is the words of someone else.

101

If a child says to the mother, "Daddy doesn't love me anymore, does he?" the thoughtful mother will respond, "Why do you say that, darling?" After the child has expressed disappointments, the mother might ask, "In what ways would you like Daddy to show his love to you?" The answer to that question should be communicated to the father, not in a condemning way, but as information. To the father or mother who has left I would say, "You have divorced your spouse. Please do not divorce your children." They need your love.

A second emotional need for the child is discipline. A child needs boundaries in order to feel secure. Sometimes a divorced parent will unconsciously try to make up for the child's loss by indulging the child. If you give in to every wish of your child, you will soon be his servant, and he will grow up expecting others to serve him. The problem with a "king complex" (the feeling that everyone is expected to serve you) is that there are not many openings for kings in our society. The parent who raises a "king" is raising a misfit.

Your child needs the security of restrictions. If both parents can agree on basic patterns of conduct, so much the better. Such things as bedtime, how much and what type of television programs, candy allowance, study habits, piano practice, and table manners can easily be agreed upon by parents who take seriously the task of raising a responsible child. When standards are different in the two places of residence the child may enjoy the greater freedom granted by one parent, but he will lose the security of firm boundaries. If you cannot agree with your spouse on certain boundaries, then at least be consistent in your differences. Don't constantly change your own rules. Such inconsistency is emotionally frustrating to the child.

A common pitfall among divorced parents is that of allowing their own emotional needs to govern their actions toward the children. For example, a parent might utilize exorbitant gift-giving to win the love of the child and thus meet his own need to be loved. Or, one parent might constantly belittle the other in front of the child in order to vent hostility toward the ex-spouse. Such parading of each other's failures does not help the child. We must analyze our actions to ascertain their purpose. The well-being of the child must be the objective standard by which we judge our behavior.

In the early days of separation the resident parent should seek to keep the children's routine as normal as possible. When feasible, the resident parent and children should remain in the house or apartment for at least several months. The divorce is traumatic enough. Moving to new surroundings, leaving friends, changing schools simply compound the feelings of insecurity in the child. If a move is necessary, however, try to maintain as many of the old established patterns of living as possible. Such things as reading stories, playing games, and praying together bring warm feelings even in a strange place.

The resident parent should welcome the involvement of the nonresident parent in the lives of the children. Most divorce settlements will give guidelines for the nonresident parent's time with the children. It is important to remember that both individuals are still parents, and though roles are changed, both should have ongoing relationships with the children. Exceptions to that may be when one parent is physically or emotionally unable to relate constructively to the children. In such cases, the resident parent may want to seek counsel from a lawyer or counselor as to how to respond to their particular situation.

Friends, relatives, and the church family can be of inestimable value to the children of divorced parents. Grandfathers can serve as role models when the father, for whatever reason, is unable to spend time with children. Aunts and uncles are sometimes willing to have the children for extended visits. Friends may be able to spend quality time with the children and teach them specific skills. More and more churches are beginning to respond to the needs of the single parent. Workshops, seminars, books, tapes, and personal counseling are now available in many churches. Don't hesitate to ask friends and relatives to help if you think they are capable of doing so. Many are willing, but will hesitate to take the initiative.

Living in a divorced home is not ideal for children, but then, much of life must be lived in a less than ideal setting. Be positive. Make the most of what you have. Put your hand in the hand of God; reach out for available help. Let the love of God comfort you and the power of God enable you to be the best possible single parent.

AM I FREE TO REMARRY?

It is beyond the scope of this book to give a lengthy treatise of the biblical passages dealing with divorce and remarriage. A number of excellent books are available that give a detailed exegetical analysis of those passages (see Appendix). The Bible emphasizes God's ideal: monogamous marriage for life. It speaks of divorce as man's failure to experience the ideal, but it says very little about remarriage. As George W. Peters, noted New Testament scholar says, "The God who promulgates the highest and noblest ideals cannot legislate lower and lesser ideals, though He may permit man to live and to operate on a subideal level."[3]

Even in the case of widows and widowers, the Bible neither commands nor forbids remarriage. The choice is left to the individual as he seeks to discern what is best for him (Romans 7:1-6; 1 Corinthians 7:6-9; 1 Timothy 5:14). In the case of divorce because of fornication or desertion, again the Bible is silent about remarriage. Dr. Peters notes:

"There is nothing in the words of Christ in Matthew 5:32 and 19:1-9 that forbids remarriage of people divorced because of fornication. Christ does not even reflect negatively upon remarriage in such cases. Neither is there legislation in the writings of the apostles (specifically, Paul in 1 Corinthians 7:15) that would make remarriage of a deserted believer sinful."[4]

Thus, in the case of divorce because of fornication or desertion, many believe the Bible does not condemn or commend remarriage.

Divorce does take place for reasons other than sexual unfaithfulness and desertion, however. With the rise of no-fault divorce laws, most divorces grow out of very subjective reasons, like supposed noncompatibility. Remarriage of those divorced for causes other than fornication and desertion constitutes adultery according to the statements of Christ and Paul (Matthew 5:32, 19:9; Mark 10:11-12; Luke 16:18; 1 Corinthians 7:15). Paul says in 1 Corinthians 7:10-11, "To the married I give instructions, not I, but the Lord, that a wife should not leave her husband (but if she does leave, let her remain unmarried, or else be reconciled to her husband), and that the husband should not [divorce] his wife."

Although the possibility of divorce is recognized, it is never encouraged in Scripture. Remarriage, except possibly when the divorce is based upon fornication or desertion, is always seen as adultery. Immediately, the question is raised, Cannot adultery be forgiven? The answer is clearly yes. If there is genuine confession of sin, adultery can be forgiven. Forgiveness, however, does not erase all the results of sin. Thousands of forgiven couples will testify of the ever-present scars that are never fully erased.

Should you remarry? Why not put that question on the shelf until you have made every effort at reconciliation? If reconciliation is impossible—if the divorce is finalized, if your spouse has remarried, or has been sexually unfaithful and refuses all attempts at reconciliation—you may consider remarriage. But do not move too fast. Most counselors agree that it takes about two years to work through the emotional trauma of a divorce. The most common pitfall is premature remarriage. That perhaps accounts for the fact that the divorce rate of second marriages is higher than that of first marriages. Take more time to prepare for your second marriage. Unity will be more difficult to obtain because of the frustrations and memories you bring to the second marriage. Rediscover yourself before you seek remarriage.

GROWTH ASSIGNMENTS

1. If your spouse insists on divorce and refuses to take any steps toward reconciliation, ask God to give you strength and wisdom in accepting this decision.

2. Keep the door of reconciliation open from your side and pray that God will continue to stimulate the mind of your spouse.
3. Seek to be equitable in all legal arrangements.
4. Seek the counsel of a lawyer, a pastor, or a friend in the areas in which you have questions.
5. Select one or more of the books or tapes from the resources listed in the Appendix of this volume, and continue seeking personal growth.

NOTES

1. Howard L. Bass, *Divorce or Marriage: A Legal Guide* (Englewood Cliffs, N.J.: Prentice-Hall, 1976), p. 179.
2. Mel Krantzler, *Creative Divorce* (New York: New American Library, 1975), p. 220.
3. George W. Peters, *Divorce and Remarriage* (Chicago: Moody, 1970), p. 21.
4. Ibid., p. 22.

11

Facing the Future

" 'For I know the plans that I have for you,' declares the LORD, 'plans for welfare and not for calamity to give you a future and a hope' " (Jeremiah 29:11). Contrary to your present feelings, your future can be bright. God's plans for you are good. Past failures need not destroy your hope for the future. If you choose, you can discover the elation of a marriage reborn—reborn on a much deeper level than before. Your communication and understanding of each other can be much more intimate than you have ever known. As you forgive the past, share feelings, find understanding, and learn to love each other, you can find fulfillment in your marriage. That is not wishful thinking. It has become reality for hundreds of couples who have committed themselves to walk the road to reconciliation.

I have tried to be realistic as I have described the process of restoring a marriage. It is not easy. It will be painful as your mate communicates honest feelings that have developed through the years. You will have the tendency to defend yourself and deny that you have not met needs. You will see clearly the failures of your spouse whereas your own will seem insignificant. It is hard to admit that you have also failed your spouse.

As both of you understand your failures and move to correct them, you can experience tremendous personal growth. Some of the things you have disliked about yourself through the years can be changed. You are not a slave to old patterns of behavior. You will be greatly encouraged as you see yourself becoming the loving, thoughtful person you want to be. You will be excited about the positive changes you see in your spouse.

Such change is not likely to happen without the help of God. You both need to return to God in a fresh way and invite Him into your lives. Christ died to pay the penalty for your past sins. God wants to forgive. He will not hold the past against you, if you will accept Christ as your Savior. The Spirit of God will come to live with you and give you power to make needed changes in your life. With His help, you can accomplish things you never dreamed possible. Your whole life can be turned around, and in turn you can help others. I want to challenge you to accept God's forgiveness, open the door of your life to Christ, and with your hand in God's hand, move out to attempt the things suggested in this book. You will never regret your attempts to accomplish God's best.

As I have tried to say throughout this volume, your efforts do not guarantee the restoration of your marriage. Your spouse has the freedom to turn away from all your overtures. If, after you make every effort at reconciliation, your spouse refuses to be reconciled, where does that leave you? It leaves you with your hand in God's hand. That is not a bad position. You will be free from the guilt of past failures, because you will have confessed your wrong to God and to your spouse. You will have the satisfaction of having sought reconciliation. Your relationship with God will be vital and growing. You will appreciate your own abilities and admit your weaknesses. You will be on a program of personal growth and ministry that will lead to fulfillment. God will not hold you responsible for the decision of your spouse. You are only responsible for your own attitudes and behavior.

If reconciliation is not possible, do not think that God's purposes for you are over. God has gifted you and called you to serve in His family. He wants to use your life for positive purposes, and He wants to meet all of your needs (Philippians 4:19). Don't say, "I can never be happy without my spouse." If your spouse will not return, God will still lead you from the valley of despair to the mountain of joy. God is not through with you. Your happiness is not dependent upon the behavior of your spouse, but upon your response to God and life. "I can do all things through [Christ] who strengthens me" (Philippians 4:13). "For it is God who is at work in you, both to will and to work for His good pleasure" (Philippians 2:13).

The highest goal in life is to follow God's leadership daily. God will not only show you the way to walk, but He will give the power to take the necessary steps. He will use friends, books, tapes, and the church to help you. In those hours when no one else can help, He will assure you of His presence. As David said, "Thou wilt make known to me the path of life; in Thy presence is fulness of joy; in Thy right hand there are pleasures forever" (Psalms 16:11).

The hymnwriter expressed the incomprehensible joy of yielding oneself to God when he said:

> I have found a deep peace that I never had known
> And a joy this world cannot afford,
> Since I yielded control of my body and soul
> To my wonderful, wonderful Lord!

> Haldor Lillenas, "My Wonderful Lord"

In the privacy of our own hearts, no one can ever destroy the deep peace that is the result of knowing God as Father. Nothing could bring more security. No human relationship can replace our need for sharing life with God. He in turn will lead us in developing human relationships in which we can love and be loved by others.

THE POWER OF CHOICE

The future is intended to be the brightest portion of your life. Don't spoil it by allowing your feelings to pull you into a debilitating depression. Don't allow bitterness to consume your spirit. Don't destroy yourself with self-pity. Don't drive your

109

friends away by constantly refusing their comfort or by playing your recording of gloom. The Bible is filled with examples of individuals who found their greatest success after experiencing tremendous failures.

You can follow the road of self-destruction and end up with an emotional breakdown. You can make your life miserable by making each day a rerun of the past. Or you can say with the psalmist, "This is the day which the LORD has made; let us rejoice and be glad in it" (Psalm 118:24). You may not be able to rejoice over the past or even over your present situation, but you can rejoice that God has given you the ability to use this day for good. When you do, you will be glad.

Don't try to live all of your future today. Jesus emphasized the importance of living one day at a time. "Do not be anxious then, saying, 'What shall we eat?' or 'With what shall we clothe ourselves?' . . . for your heavenly Father knows that you need all these things. But seek first His kingdom and His righteousness; and all these things shall be added to you. Therefore do not be anxious for tomorrow; for tomorrow will care for itself. Each day has enough trouble of its own" (Matthew 6:31-34). You will probably agree that you have all the trouble you can handle today. Therefore, don't spend time today worrying about the problems that will arise tomorrow. Spend your time working on present problems.

What can I do today that will improve my situation? What do I need to pray about today? With whom do I need to talk today? What action do I need to take today? The answers to those questions will lead to constructive activity today. Your total responsibility to God is to make the best use of this day. You cannot undo the past. The future is tentative. God has entrusted to you only the present, and wise use of today is all that He expects. Your total life cannot be straightened out today. Work on cleaning up one corner of your life. Choose the corner that you think is most important right now.

PLANNING YOUR DAY

I have found it extremely helpful to plan each day before I

begin. After all, time is life. When I plan my time, I am planning my life. Each hour is a portion of my life. Under God's direction, I am responsible for my use of it. Therefore, at the beginning of each day I take pencil and paper in hand and ask God to guide my thoughts as I plan my day. I list everything that I think needs to be done that day: phone calls I need to make, letters I need to write, visits I need to make, books and magazines I need to read, things I need to get, places I need to go, information I need to find, activities I need to attend. Once those are listed, I ask God to help me decide which are most important. I go back and number each item according to importance. Then I begin by doing the most important thing first, or if it must be done during a certain time framework, I block that time out on my schedule first. Then I proceed to number 2. I may not finish my list, but at least I get the most important things for that day accomplished. The others I can put on my list tomorrow, if tomorrow comes.

That kind of planning and follow-through helps us accomplish the most with each day of life. The greatest enemy of success in life will be laziness or apathy toward your time. If you simply sit around watching television, waiting for something to happen, your life will be wasted. If you sit around feeling sorry for yourself, you may still be sitting ten years from now. If, however, you make the most of today and every day, you will accomplish God's will for your life.

You are responsible for what you do with your life. No one else can take that responsibility. You can blame others for your unhappiness, but it is a hollow claim. God will not hold you responsible for what others do or fail to do toward you. He will only hold you responsible for what you do with your life. You cannot determine other's actions, but you can choose your reactions. You do not have to be miserable simply because someone has mistreated you. You may not be able to control your immediate feelings, but you can certainly determine your behavior. Plan your life and follow your plan.

Be certain that you include God in your planning. You may

want to begin your planning each day with the words of the
song writer:

> Jesus, Saviour, pilot me
> Over life's tempestuous sea;
> Unknown waves before me roll,
> Hiding rock and treach'rous shoal;
> Chart and compass come from Thee;
> Jesus, Saviour, pilot me.

Edward Hopper, "Jesus, Saviour, Pilot Me"

That verse may well express your feelings as you face the un-
certainties of the future. God knows your feelings and does not
condemn you for them. He does, however, expect you to make
the most of your life in spite of your feelings. Plan your time
and go against your feelings if necessary to accomplish the
things you feel need to be done today. You may come to the
end of the day exhausted, but you will have the satisfaction of
having done something constructive. As the days come and go,
you will feel less and less a victim of your circumstances. You
will be demonstrating to yourself that with God's help, your life
can be productive and fulfilling.

Read Your Way to Health

Whether you are able to move down the road of reconciliation, or you are forced to accept divorce, reading the right books
can be a tremendous aid in helping you make the most of life.
In the Appendix of this volume you will find a brief description of several books designed to help you. You may not agree
with all you read but look for practical ideas that may assist you
in accomplishing your goals. God has not left us without direction. Books written from a biblical perspective can help you
find God's way. Remember, it is not enough just to read. You
must apply truth to life. You may need to make radical changes
in your present thinking and behavior. If so, you have all of
God's power to aid you.

112

GROWTH ASSIGNMENTS

Begin the rest of your life by planning today!

THINGS TO DO . . . TODAY

Date_____

Order of
Importance   *Completed*

○ _____ ☐

○ _____ ☐

○ _____ ☐

○ _____ ☐

○ _____ ☐

○ _____ ☐

○ _____ ☐

○ _____ ☐

○ _____ ☐

○ _____ ☐

○ _____ ☐

○ _____ ☐

1. List the specific things you need to accomplish today.
2. Number them in order of importance by placing the num-

ber *1* in the circle by the item you feel is most important, the number *2* by the second most important, and so on.

3. When you finish a particular task, put a check ($\checkmark$) in the block to the right.

Appendix

RESOURCES FOR GROWING WHILE SEPARATED

Bustanoby, Andre. *You Can Change Your Personality*. Grand Rapids: Zondervan, 1976.
Written for both counselor and layman, this book provides help in developing an adaptive, well-balanced personality. Bustanoby describes eight personality types and indicates steps to change those aspects of one's personality that are troublesome. The book is geared toward personal understanding and growth rather than marriage.

Carroll, Anne Kristin. *From the Brink of Divorce*. Garden City, N.Y.: Doubleday, Galilee, 1978.
With a strong emphasis on the power of Christ to change lives, Mrs. Carroll tells her own story of coming from the brink of divorce. She shares the seven most common marital difficulties: self-centeredness, failure to accept one's mate as he or she is, poor communication, negative feelings about oneself, sex problems, assumption of improper roles by husband and wife, and, most importantly, failure to apply Christian principles in the marriage. This book is written with genuine understanding and sympathy for those who are separated.

Johnson, James. *Loneliness Is Not Forever*. Chicago: Moody, 1979.
The strong message of this book is that loneliness does not have to cripple, causing despair, bitterness, illness, and death. "No child of God should ever allow loneliness to dictate the course of his or her life."

Landorf, Joyce. *His Stubborn Love*. Grand Rapids: Zondervan, 1971.

This book is a first-person account of a dying marriage and how it survived. Joyce Landorf reveals the personal struggle through which she and her husband, Dick, walked. She portrays the reality of a broken relationship and shares answers that led to a joyful and healing resolution. This book offers encouragement to those who have lost hope.

McGinnis, Alan Loy. *The Friendship Factor: How to Get Closer to the People You Care For*. Minneapolis: Augsburg, 1979.

This book is a must for couples who want to become friends. It is filled with ideas on how to deepen relationships, cultivate intimacy, handle negative emotions, and forgive. The section on salvaging a faltering friendship has particular application to those who are separated.

Miles, Herbert J. *Sexual Understanding Before Marriage*. Grand Rapids: Zondervan, 1971.

Though directed to those who have never married, this book has an excellent section on controlling the sexual drive while single. The principles of sexual control would be the same for those who are separated. Dr. Miles's treatment of masturbation and the case for chastity outside of marriage will be of special interest to those who are separated. For practical help on following the biblical pattern of sexual control, this book is invaluable.

Wood, Britton. *Single Adults Want to Be the Church, Too*. Nashville: Broadman, 1977.

Britton Wood was the first full-time minister for singles in his denomination. His book is especially valuable to pastors and other church leaders who want their singles ministry to include the "single again." He shares some pitfalls to avoid and offers insights and ideas for programming effectively with single adults.

RESOURCES FOR REBUILDING A MARRIAGE

Chapman, Gary D. *Toward a Growing Marriage*. Chicago: Moody, 1979.

Once you make the decision to seek reconciliation, this book will point the way to marital growth. Your marriage does not have to be locked into any situation simply because "that's the way we've always done it." You can find new patterns of living that will lead to marital unity. This book makes biblical principles practical and easy to apply to daily life. Each chapter concludes with specific "growth assignments" designed to help you get the truth into life.

Chapman, Gary D. *Toward a Growing Marriage Seminar.* A cassette program. Marriage Seminar, P.O. Box 10285, Winston-Salem, N.C. 27108.

These cassettes contain seven hours of counsel on how to build a Christian marriage. Recorded before a live audience, this seminar is filled with humor and illustrations of practical biblical truth as it relates to daily life. Much of the material found in *Toward a Growing Marriage,* listed above, is included. These tapes are especially valuable for those who prefer listening rather than reading.

Dahl, Gerald L. *Why Christian Marriages Are Breaking Up.* Nashville: Nelson, 1979.

This book is a thorough examination of the marriage vows and offers practical help on how you can enjoy keeping those vows. Especially insightful chapters are "How to Have an Affair with the Person You Married" and "Understanding How to Be a 'Submissive' Husband."

Miles, Herbert J. *Sexual Happiness in Marriage.* Grand Rapids: Zondervan, 1967.

This book contains frank, honest discussion about the role of sex in Christian marriage. Attitudes and techniques essential to sexual compatibility are carefully presented including: the male and female anatomy, the dynamics of love play, planned parenthood, and causes of sexual frustration. This volume is recommended for couples who need to grow in sexual unity.

Swihart, Judson J. *How Do You Say, "I Love You"?* Downers Grove, Ill.: Inter-Varsity, 1977.

This volume is one of the most useful tools available for learning how to meet your spouse's emotional need for love. He discusses eight basic "love languages" and gives inventories to help you discover your "love language." The book speaks to one of the biggest hindrances to marital unity—failure to understand what makes your mate feel loved. It is a must for those who seek to restore marital oneness.

117

Swindoll, Charles R. *Strike the Original Match*. Portland: Multnomah, 1980.

From his rich experience as a pastor, the author has written about how to rekindle and preserve your marriage fire. His advice is soundly biblical, yet written with the freshness of today that we have come to expect from Charles Swindoll.

Wheat, Ed. *Sex Techniques and Sex Problems in Marriage*. A cassette program. Springdale, Ark.: Scriptural Counsel, 1975.

These cassettes provide three hours of intimate sexual counsel from a Christian family physician. This tape program contains much of the same material found in *Intended for Pleasure*, listed below, and will be especially helpful to those who prefer listening rather than reading.

Wheat, Ed, and Wheat, Gaye. *Intended for Pleasure*. Old Tappan, N.J.: Revell, 1977.

As a Christian family physician, Dr. Wheat and his wife have identified common sexual problems and given practical help. This volume is fast becoming the standard reference book on sex from a Christian perspective. It provides not only sound medical advice but also helpful insights into the emotional and spiritual aspects of lovemaking.

RESOURCES FOR COPING WITH DIVORCE

Crook, Roger H. *An Open Book to the Christian Divorcee*. Nashville: Broadman, 1974.

Dr. Crook writes with a strong commitment to the biblical ideal of reconciliation. He asks some very probing questions of those considering divorce. If divorce does occur, however, he gives practical help on the questions most often asked by the divorcee. He includes topics such as: emotional stresses, the children, relating to the opposite sex, legal matters, and church life.

Hensley, J. Clark. *Coping with Being Single Again*. Nashville: Broadman, 1978.

Dr. Hensley offers genuine help in coping with grief, loneliness, boredom, health and money matters, sexual needs, and single parenting. It is an excellent book for those who, because of divorce, must face being single again.

Peters, George W. *Divorce and Remarriage*. Chicago: Moody, 1970.
This book addresses briefly but thoroughly the biblical passages
that speak to the divorce and remarriage issue. Written by a biblical scholar, but in language that all can understand, it will be
especially helpful to those who have questions about the biblical
stance on remarriage.

Smoke, Jim. *Growing Through Divorce*. Irvine, Calif.: Harvest
    House, 1976.
When reconciliation is impossible and divorce a reality, this book
points the way to life beyond divorce. It is a very practical book
dealing with such subjects as: assuming responsibility for yourself, finding a family, finding forgiveness, your children, your
future, and new life.

Watts, Virginia. *The Single Parent*. Old Tappan, N.J.: Revell, 1977.
Out of her own struggles as a single parent Virginia Watts has
written a very readable and helpful book. Her ideas on how to
meet children's emotional needs are especially insightful. A section on accepting and responding creatively to your own emotions
is included.

Moody Press, a ministry of the Moody Bible Institute, is designed for education, evangelization, and edification. If we may assist you in knowing more about Christ and the Christian life, please write us without obligation: Moody Press, c/o MLM, Chicago, Illinois 60610.